6-22-00

To Cookie,
Thanks for the kindness
you extended to Dad and our
family. Best of health. We love you!

"BULLET BOB" COMES TO LOUISVILLE

"BULLET BOB" COMES TO LOUISVILLE—
and Other Tales from a Baseball Life

BY JOHN MORRIS

FOREWORD BY WILLIE McGEE

DIAMOND COMMUNICATIONS, INC.
SOUTH BEND, INDIANA
1999

"BULLET BOB" COMES TO LOUISVILLE—
and Other Tales from a Baseball Life
Copyright © 1999 by John Morris

10 9 8 7 6 5 4 3 2 1

Manufactured in the United States of America

Diamond Communications, Inc.
Post Office Box 88
South Bend, Indiana 46624-0088
Editorial: (219) 299-9278
Fax: (219) 299-9296
Orders Only: 1-800-480-3717
Website: www.diamondbooks.com

Library of Congress Cataloging-in-Publication Data

Morris, John, 1961-
    "Bullet Bob" comes to Louisville--and other tales from a base-
ball life / by John Morris; foreword by Willie McGee.
        p.   cm.
    ISBN 1-888698-20-9
    1. Morris, John, 1961-   . 2. Baseball players--United States-
-Biography.   I. Title.
    GV865.M65A3   1999
    796.357'092--dc21
    [B]   98-30818
                                                            CIP

CONTENTS

FOREWORD

I first met John Morris, a.k.a. "Johnny Mo," during the 1986 spring training in St. Petersburg, Florida. I had already been with the St. Louis Cardinals for five seasons while this kid from Long Island, New York, was in his first camp with the team. The year before we had traded an established major leaguer named Lonnie Smith to the Kansas City Royals for John, so I figured this kid had to have some talent. It didn't take long to find out I was right. John had all the tools you wanted to see in a young player—good speed, a strong arm, and a quick bat.

During the first week of camp, I studied his every move. The more I watched John the more I saw a young man with tremendous physical talent, a great attitude, and a tireless work ethic. Over the next six weeks, the foundation of a solid friendship, one that still exists today, was built.

John and I were both outfielders, so we spent a good deal of time together on the field. Whether we were shagging flyballs, taking batting practice, or running wind sprints, the two of us supported and encouraged one another.

Unfortunately, at the tail end of spring training John was optioned to Triple-A Louisville to begin the season. I figured it was just a matter of time before he would be promoted to the parent club. Fortunately, I was right. From August of 1986 through the summer of 1990 we were teammates in St. Louis. I'm happy to say that some of my fondest baseball memories, including a trip to the 1987 World Series, came with Johnny Mo at my side.

I was honored and excited when John approached me about writing the foreword to *"Bullet Bob" Comes to Louisville.* My excitement continued to grow after reading his entire manuscript. The 22 stories that he has compiled are fascinating baseball stories that provide valuable lessons in the game of baseball and the game of life. These tales cover a 15-year period and are brilliantly presented over the course of a nine-inning game.

Every player who has ever stepped between the white lines of a ballpark has dreams of someday making it to the major leagues. Along the way, players are bound to experience moments of glory coupled with periods of agony and despair. I laughed out loud when I read about John's minor league days with the Royals and the Cardinals. Although we never played minor league ball together, I appreciate what happened to him in "The Twin Bill from Hell" and "The Pancake Man." These hilarious minor league stories remind me of my younger days coming up in the New York Yankees' organization. They provide an accurate portrayal of life "in the bushes."

Some of the more intimate stories in this collection include "The Best Seat in the House" and "Mother's Day." "The Best Seat in the House" is a touching story about John's relationship with his father. John's return to the Cardinals following his dad's funeral gives the team and the fans of St. Louis a huge lift during the heat of a pennant race and the hardest three days of his life. "Mother's Day" is one of the most incredible stories I've ever read. It was very emotional for me because I knew Grace Morris well, and because I knew of John's struggles during his 1991 season with the Phillies. This story will bring tears to your eyes.

"Gentlemen's Quarterly" and "Three-Man Dead Lift" examine some of the more creative practical jokes in baseball. John, with the help of his teammates, exposes the egos and attitudes of Joe Magrane and Howard Hilton in these hysterical stories. In "GQ" John paints a vivid picture of Joe's overwhelming desire to have his face on the pages of the popular fashion magazine, and how his oversized ego prevented him from distinguishing fantasy from reality. "Three-Man Dead Lift" is a great story about Howard Hilton and his desire to be in the middle of everything. His teammates go to great lengths to make sure he isn't disappointed.

"My Aching Back" and "One Last Try" deal with the issues of injury, adversity, and retirement. They are stories of how John overcame serious injuries to his back that jeopardized not only his baseball career, but his life as well. The issue of retirement from baseball, the most difficult and personal issue a player will ever confront, is also addressed.

To John Morris, *"Bullet Bob" Comes to Louisville* is more than just a title of a book. What makes his stories so compelling is they deal with everyday life. When kids play baseball today in their backyard, some might pretend to be Mark McGwire or Roger Clemens. But when adversity and triumph came calling, it was John's courage and tenacity that made him the one worth imitating.

"Bullet Bob" Comes to Louisville is a hard-hitting look at Johnny Mo's struggles and triumphs in and out of the game of baseball. It will make you laugh and it will make you cry. John has come full circle from a man who overcame serious obstacles and setbacks to a man who empowers lives. His stories are ones of a champion.

Willie McGee

(Photo © St. Louis Baseball Cardinals)

A portion of the proceeds from the sale of this book will be given to Christ of the Hills—a Christian community of healing and human growth in upstate New York for young men ages 16-25 who suffer the effects of addiction, indolence, or other rebellion. It is a school in the larger life-sense where people are restored and invited to wholeness through the struggle, discipline, and balance of prayer, work, and recreation in a small, non-violent community.

PREFACE

My roots are in the game of baseball. From the time I was a Little Leaguer until the time I retired from professional baseball at the age of 35, I had many different thoughts about the game. As a matter of fact, some of my fondest baseball images grace the cover of this book. I remember spending countless hours as an eight-year-old imitating the drop-and-drive pitching style of Tom Seaver. During my teenage years I listened as my dad told stories about his semi-pro playing days with the New York Red Sox. Most of them made me wonder what his life was like as a vibrant young man during the Roaring Twenties. And my days as an aggressive minor leaguer in search of major league success are forever etched in my mind.

When I came up with the idea to write this collection of vignettes, I wanted the reader to have a greater understanding of the humorous, emotionally charged, and often chaotic lifestyle that professional baseball players lead. Most baseball fans usually only see game scores and highlights on television, hear plays on the radio, or read about their favorite players in the newspapers. Rarely do they get a chance to see the human side of baseball or learn about the long, often difficult road to the major leagues.

Some of the stories in *"Bullet Bob" Comes to Louisville* are humorous, others serious, but all provide a rare, down-to-earth look inside the lives of players, coaches, friends, and families. I share them out of a personal passion for baseball, both as player and fan, and in an effort to help fans rekindle their love of, and restore their faith in, the greatest game in the world.

John Mart

ACKNOWLEDGMENTS

Special thanks are extended to my brother Rich Morris, whose generous time and creative self-expression made this project possible. My sincere thanks and appreciation go to Roger Fry and Kristen Noakes Fry for their incredible coaching, editorial, and technical expertise. The staff of the Baseball Hall of Fame in Cooperstown, New York, was extremely helpful to me during the research for the book. Thank you to Temple Hayes, Caroline Carney, and Emilie Herman for encouraging me to move forward with the idea of a short story format. And to Jim and Jill Langford for their vision and their willingness to publish this collection.

A SPECIAL THANK YOU...

To my wife Linda—for your patience and support during all the ups and downs. Over the years, your courage and persistence, along with your endless search to find an answer to your physical challenges, have inspired me. Thanks to your spirit we now have a new life together. I thank you from the bottom of my heart for introducing us to Nikken, and for helping me leave the baseball industry with my love and affection for it intact.

Special thanks also go to Putter and Sharky, our four-legged furry friends. Thank you, Putter, for hanging out on my lap during all the early morning writing sessions. And to Sharky for your willingness to knock dozens of pencils off my desk at any given moment.

To my loving family—
Mom and Dad, my wife Linda,
and my brothers and sisters—
Richard, Stephen, Joan, Karen, and Andrew

"It's a great day for a ballgame; let's play two."

—Ernie Banks

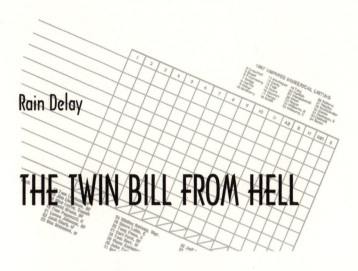

Rain Delay

THE TWIN BILL FROM HELL

THE STORM HAD APPEARED from nowhere. Dark clouds had quickly gathered and the sky unleashed a torrent of thunder, lightning, and rain—just in time to delay the start of the first game of the double-header.

Having recently signed my first professional baseball contract in July 1982, I was assigned to the Fort Myers Royals of the Florida State League—the Kansas City Royals' Class-A affiliate. I'd heard all the stories about the glamour and glory of professional baseball, and looked forward to playing before huge crowds of adoring fans. Unfortunately, no one had prepared me for baseball's more difficult and frustrating moments.

Our team began an eight-game homestand against the Fort Lauderdale Yankees—a team that possessed the best record in the Florida bush league. I had arrived at the park at 2 P.M. and we went through our daily routine of batting and infield practice. By 6 that evening, the scheduled start of the twinbill's first game, I was enthusiastic and confident in my place in the lineup playing center field. I was eager to get

1

started, but like everyone else in the park, I sat and waited for the storm to pass.

The rain stopped at 7:30. The umpires decided that the game would begin at 8:30, allowing plenty of time to ready the field. A sparse crowd of about 100 people fidgeted in the stands. So much for the huge, cheering crowds I'd expected.

The early stages of the first game proved to be a pitchers' duel between two of the better pitchers in the league. The score was knotted at 1-1 as we entered the sixth inning. Suddenly, the Yankees erupted with four runs to take a commanding lead. After that, the pace of the game bogged down. Poor pitching led to lots of free passes and long innings. Meanwhile, the rain started again and was coming down as a slow drizzle.

By the bottom of the ninth inning, the outlook for the home team was bleak. We were down to our last turn at-bat when we managed to load the bases. Miraculously, our cleanup hitter, Willie Neal, connected for a game-tying grandslam—sending the game into extra innings. We dragged into the 12th inning before winning on a two-out single. Final score: 8-7 for the good guys.

The first game had taken three and a half hours to play, finally ending at midnight. We were scheduled to be back on the field in 20 minutes to begin game number two. We were tired—and so were the fans. Of the 100 or so spectators who had been in the stands for the first game, about two dozen staunch supporters remained—and even they appeared to be having difficulty staying awake.

Under normal conditions, most umpiring crews would have postponed the second game until the following day. However, knowing this was the last time we were scheduled to face the Yankees that season, our umpires—gung-ho and fresh from umpiring school—were determined to stick to the letter of the law.

We got set to take the field at 12:25, but another thunderstorm pounded the area. The first pitch had yet to be thrown and already we were in a holding pattern. Fifteen minutes later, the rain eased and we took our positions at 12:45.

Between games of The Twin Bill From Hell, July 1982, Fort Myers, FL. (Photo by Rich Morris)

3

Our pitcher, Nick Harsh, wound up and delivered the first pitch of the game. The Yankee batter hacked at the hanging curveball, sending a screaming line drive back at Harsh. The lanky righthander threw up his arm to defend himself, but the ball hit him squarely on his hand, fracturing it badly. A 15-minute delay ensued while another pitcher was brought in and warmed up.

It is now an hour into the next day and we were still in the top of the first. Our new pitcher was Tony Ferreira, a hard-throwing lefty. Ferreira threw his first pitch over the outside corner for strike one. Getting the ball back, Ferreira quickly got his sign from the catcher. He went into the stretch. Suddenly, the 357 G.E. mercury-vapor lamps surrounding the field flickered once, and went out. There we were, nine position players, three umpires, two base coaches, and an opposing hitter standing on a field cloaked in total darkness. At this point, we were an hour into the second game and the first batter had yet to be retired.

I was convinced that the game could not possibly go on. After all, we had a legitimate excuse to discontinue this fiasco, didn't we? But our groundskeeper—short, rumpled, and looking like he hadn't shaved in several days—appeared from somewhere and convinced the umpires that he could have the lights back on in only a few minutes. We waited in our dugout, wandering around in the darkness and cracking stupid jokes.

It took a half-hour, but power was finally restored. The umpires beckoned us onto the field. It was now 1:30, raining, and only about a dozen die-hard fans remained in the stadium, but the umpires were determined that the "show must go on." My brother Rich had flown down from New Jersey and was among those persevering until the final out. His loyalty was admirable but it couldn't keep him from nodding off on occasion.

As I stood in center field, the vision of playing baseball in a grave-yard flashed across my mind. Except for a hum from the lights and the occasional whining of a mosquito, it was deadly silent. A light mist hovered near the ground. The light rain soaked everything and everyone. Huddled in their seats, the fans were still and eerily silent. I wondered if they were asleep—and couldn't blame them if they were.

Tony Ferreira took his warm-up pitches. The game was ready to resume. The homeplate umpire pointed at the pitcher and commanded "Play Ball!" A split second later, he screamed, "Time Out!" Waving his arms, he leapt from behind homeplate shouting at no one in particular, "All right. What's going on here? Who stole second base?" We all looked to the middle of the diamond. Second base was nowhere to be seen.

As far as I was concerned, this was the last straw. Slamming my glove on the ground, I turned to look at my fellow outfielders. Suddenly, out of the corner of my eye, I noticed something moving about 20 yards beyond the left-center field fence. A shadowy figure of a small boy raced down the street with our second base firmly tucked under his arm and two stadium security guards behind him in hot pursuit. It looked like the Keystone Cops chasing Boy Wonder. As they disappeared into the mist, I found myself cheering for the boy, hoping that the theft of second base would finally end our misery.

Without second base, I was sure the game was over. Unfortunately, our little buddy, the groundskeeper, surfaced again. He informed the umpires that he had another base stored in an equipment shed located at the far end of the complex—a quarter mile away. We waited while he slowly ambled toward the shed, eventually returning with a new sack. At this rate, there was no telling when I might get my first at-bat. The steady drizzle was not heavy enough to discontinue play, but was enough to be annoying. My spikes were soaked and full of mud—each foot must have weighed five extra pounds.

By 2 A.M., the new base was firmly installed, and the game resumed again. It lingered on as an ugly affair, littered with many walks, errors, and poor defensive plays—mainly due to the weariness of the players. Fortunately, we played without any more interruptions—a miracle in itself. The last out was recorded at 4:30 A.M. We won by a score of 4-3. To their credit, those same dozen fans who saw the first pitch remained right to the end. As I dragged my body off the field, I saw ushers nudging a few fans out of a deep slumber.

5

Showering and dressing quickly, I was anxious to get home. Trudging wearily across the parking lot, I opened the door of my car and plopped into the front seat. That's when I realized that some 14 hours ago, I'd forgotten to close my car windows when I'd arrived at the park. Almost as if it refused to die, the ghost of the twinbill had followed me onto the parking lot. It was back to the clubhouse to change clothes and retrieve some towels to clean up the mess.

The sky had lightened by the time I reached home, and the twinbill from hell had finally passed into the recordbooks. In a few hours, I'd have the chance to do it *all* over again!

Signing Day, July 1, 1982. From left to right: Tom Ferrick, Kansas City Royals scout; Ken Kunzman, legal rep.; Rich Morris, brother; J.M.; Mike Sheppard, head coach of Seton Hall University.

"Whitey, are we gonna eat hotdogs after the game again tonight?"
—Batboy, Aaron Herr, eight-year-old son
of second baseman Tommy, to the skipper
as the Cardinals blow a five-run lead in
the seventh inning

A Trip to the Concession Stand

THE PANCAKE MAN

FOOD WAS THE ONLY THING on my mind as our team bus meandered through the scenic foothills of the Appalachian Mountains. Our team had just swept a four-game set in Knoxville, Tennessee, and now we were headed into Chattanooga for another series. Unfortunately the Knoxville stadium concession stand had closed after the game. Our manager, Gene Lamont, decided we would wait to eat until after we arrived in Chattanooga—several hours away.

The ride between cities is all about passing time until you get to the next flea-bag motel. Team buses—the normal mode of transportation—are old, tired, and cramped. A typical road trip can last anywhere from a week to 10 days, with ride times of three to 16 hours. Players usually play cards, listen to Walkmans, or read to pass the time. With little room to spread out, decent sleep is usually not an option. Fortunately, our bus was reliable for the most part—except for the air conditioning. Many times we found ourselves traveling through the Deep South bathed in sweat and misery, wishing for a swift end to the trip and a good mechanic before the next one.

7

The summer of 1983 was my first full year of professional baseball and I was having the time of my life. Our team—the Jacksonville Suns, the Double-A affiliate of the Kansas City Royals, owned the best record in the league. I was enjoying a banner season. By the midpoint of the campaign I'd earned a .305 batting average, 10 HRs and 45 RBI, and a spot on the All-Star team.

Eventually, our bus rolled to a stop in the parking lot of the Lookout Mountain Hotel. Climbing down the bus steps I stretched and looked around. Perched on top of the highest mountain in the state, the hotel offered a panoramic view of Chattanooga's skyline, miles away from our vantage point. About a 100 feet below, the interstate snaked through tall oak trees. Unfortunately, the great view appeared to be all the hotel had to offer, as there was little else of interest nearby. But, as far as I was concerned, civilization could be a thousand miles away. I was doing what I enjoyed more than anything else—playing baseball.

Dropping my bags in room 105, I looked out the window, searching for a nearby place to eat. Meal money was $12 a day and the players had to fend for themselves. This usually translated into burgers, cokes, and greasy fries—the breakfast, lunch, and dinner of champions. It also meant finding places to eat within walking distance of where we were staying. If we were fortunate, gourmet dining would consist of Wendy's, McDonald's, or Taco Bell. Today we were lucky. I spotted the only restaurant in the area, a modest looking place called the Pancake Man. If any of us were going to eat, this would have to be it. Corralling my roommate, Bill Pecota, we hustled out of the hotel and across the street.

As we entered the restaurant, I laughed at the huge neon sign—a 10-foot stick figure of a man with a pancake for a face. Fully equipped with ears, eyes, nose, and a great big smile, the Pancake Man grinned at all comers. Inside, we were assaulted by the smell of frying fish and cigarette smoke. A gray haze hung low in the air. The wooden floors were badly stained and the seats were covered with worn-out upholstery. An old jukebox playing Willie Nelson's "You Were Always on My Mind" completed the scene.

Bill and I sat down at the counter. Beyond hungry, I impatiently pried open a sticky menu. The only choices that really looked appetizing were the entree selections listed on the display board overlooking the counter. I judged the $6.95 beef stew to be the safest selection in the joint.

Our waitress sidled up—an older woman with steel gray hair, horn-rimmed glasses, and a stained apron. Gaps in her teeth suggested that it had been a while since her last dental visit. I ordered the stew. While waiting for our food, I looked around and wondered about the wisdom of eating in here for the next four days. But since it was the only place near the hotel, it was either the Pancake Man or a fast. Our waitress brought the stew and I began wolfing it down.

Later, back in the hotel room, I lay on my bed watching a movie when the trouble began. A slight burning sensation in my stomach slowly worked its way into full-fledged pain. My roommate Bill lounged on his bed, devouring chips, drinking beer, and occasionally dipping into a can of Copenhagen. Every time I looked at him, the pain got worse. But my ego kept me from complaining. After all, I did *not* want to look like a timid weasel.

The lights were out minutes after the movie ended, and Bill was soon asleep. I lay curled in a fetal position feeling awful, my body wracked with pain, my insides ready to explode. Sensing the first spasm, I barely managed to stumble to the bathroom in time. What followed became a long night of hovering over the commode and listening to Bill's loud snoring.

Finally, at 4 A.M. I swallowed my pride and called the team trainer, Nick Swartz. I wanted relief and I wanted it "now." When Nick arrived, Bill awoke, wondering what the commotion was.

"Don't worry, John," said Nick. "Take these pills and you'll feel better when you wake up. If you're still sick, we'll give you the night off." These were the words I was dying to hear. The pills worked quickly; I fell asleep within the hour.

I awoke at 3 P.M. and reluctantly dressed for the ride to the stadium. Weak and wobbly-legged, I struggled up the steps of the team bus and collapsed in the nearest seat. Once in the clubhouse, I crawled onto a training table and fell asleep again within minutes. Gene Lamont woke me long enough to tell me that I was *not* in the lineup. That was music to my ears. Now, I'd have a full day to recuperate.

Unfortunately, things have a way of changing quickly in professional baseball. Fifteen minutes prior to the start of the game, Lamont again woke me, concern etched on his face. At first, I thought I was having a really bad dream. But after shaking the cobwebs from my head I knew this was the real thing.

"Johnny Mo," he said, "we have a problem. Billy Best just twisted his ankle and can't play. We're also sending Dave Leeper up to Triple-A. I need you to play right field."

Definitely not the words I wanted to hear. I looked up at him: "You're kidding, right?" But the expression on his face confirmed that he was dead serious.

"Look," he replied, "under normal circumstances, there's no way you'd play tonight. But we don't have enough players. We *need* you to play."

I rolled my eyes in disbelief. Without another word, I slid off the table and dragged my aching body in the direction of the field. Game time was just a few minutes away.

Fate, of course, had me scheduled to hit in the first inning. As I stepped into the batter's box, my body shook from dehydration and my skin was white and pasty. The bat felt like a tree trunk as I lifted it off my shoulder. Fortunately, the Chattanooga hurler, thinking I was a well-rested and finely tuned athlete, bet I'd come out looking for a fastball. Instead, he hung me a breaking ball on the first pitch. That 65-MPH mistake looked like a beach ball coming in. My sluggish bat caught up to the fat delivery, launching a towering home run over the right-field wall. Two innings later I slashed a triple into the right-center field gap. For anyone with any spring in his or her step, it would have been an inside-the-park home run.

By the fourth inning, in spite of the two hits, I was feeling worse

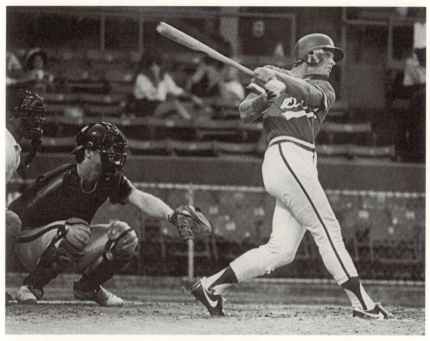

Jacksonville Suns, 1983. (Photo by Rich Morris)

than when the game began. My legs shook violently. My body felt like it had been run over by a truck. I worried that I didn't have enough energy to finish the game, but I kept my mouth shut because there was nobody to take my place.

My third and fourth at bats netted a single to center and base on balls.

Coming to the plate in the eighth inning, I found myself needing only a double to complete the "cycle." The cycle—a single, double, triple, and home run in the same game—is a rare event. I felt like hell, but knew that chances like this might not *ever* come my way again. After working the count to two balls and one strike, the Chattanooga portsider hung a slider over the middle of the plate. I laced his delivery down the right-field line and checked into second with a double. The cycle was finished—and so was I.

We had won, 10-2. I had gone 4-for-4 with six RBI. The most impressive and productive game of my early career was now complete. I

11

was proud of my accomplishment, but was completely drained of energy. My only concern was getting back to my room and going to sleep.

Moments after I dragged myself into the locker room, I found several reporters hovering around my locker. With a notable lack of enthusiasm I reluctantly fielded their questions. The beat writers picked up on my lackluster replies, their questions turning to my poor state of health. I had just finished the greatest game of my life and I couldn't enjoy it because I felt so sick. I just wanted to be left alone. Finally, the queasiness got to me and I lashed out at the reporters. Placing the blame for my illness squarely on the Pancake Man, I blasted the restaurant unmercifully.

Eventually, I got back to the hotel and slept easily that night. In the morning, I awoke feeling much better. I went in search of a local newspaper, sure there would be much praise heaped upon me for my outstanding performance the previous evening. Picking up the *Chat-*

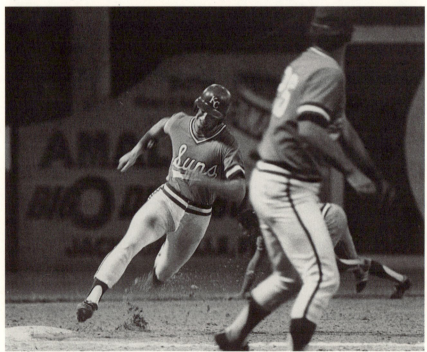

Jacksonville Suns, 1983. (Photo by Rich Morris)

tanooga Times, I turned to the sports page ready to see my name in bold letters. I did, but not quite as I had expected:

JACKSONVILLE ROCKS LOOKOUTS.
PANCAKE MAN GETS MORRIS GOING

Shaking my head in disbelief, I shouted, "You gotta be kidding me! Is this the best these pathetic newspapers can do?"

The article sang the praises of the Pancake Man, the very same eating establishment that had tried to kill me just 36 hours earlier. The sportswriter had even interviewed the manager and the chef of the Pancake Man—each man taking credit for *my* performance. Their boastful remarks indicated that it was I who should have been grateful for the opportunity to eat in such a fine establishment.

Throwing the paper to the ground in disgust, I stormed back to my room.

Later that day, I was still fuming over the ridiculous newspaper story when there was a knock at my door. Opening it, I found only an empty hallway. Just when I was about to slam the door closed, I spotted a plate of piping hot beef stew sitting on a tray on the floor. Attached to the tray was a note. I wondered who might be responsible for such a prank as I angrily snatched up the note, but as I read it, the scowl on my face was replaced by a grin. The note read:

Dear John,
Don't change a thing!
Bon Appetit.
From your loving teammates.

Picking up the tray, I closed the door and carried the food to a nearby table. Then, like any good superstitious athlete, I grabbed a spoon and ate every bit of beef stew on that plate.

Why mess with success?

"About the only problem with success is that it does not teach you how to deal with failure."

—*Tommy Lasorda*

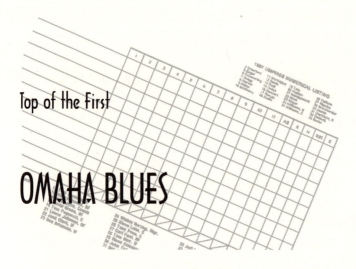

Top of the First

OMAHA BLUES

MY 1983 SEASON WITH THE Jacksonville Suns Double-A club was in the record book, and I couldn't have been happier. I'd collected 23 home runs, 92 RBI, a .288 batting average, and earned the league's Most Valuable Player honors. I was sure next season would bring a token appearance with the Triple-A club in Omaha before my major league debut with the Kansas City Royals.

Determined that 1984 was going to be my best season ever, I spent the winter months hitting and lifting weights four times a week. I also worked with a sprinting coach to improve my running speed. By the beginning of spring training, I'd increased my weight to 195, adding 10 more pounds of muscle to my already solid frame. I was a model of confidence and strength, ready to produce even better power numbers than the year before.

Rumors were circulating in the Royals' organization that several prominent players on the parent club might be suspended for illegal drug possession. This gave me another incentive to do well in the upcoming season, especially since I had been mentioned as a possible big league replacement.

Spring training began in the middle of February and I was determined to win a job as a starting outfielder for the Royals. I began swinging the bat with power and displayed vastly improved running speed in the outfield and on the basepaths. My increased arm strength allowed

Omaha Royals, 1984. (Photo by Rich Morris)

15

me to throw to all bases with power and accuracy. But as awesome as I felt from a physical fitness standpoint, I was unprepared for the daily barrage of media attention.

While dealing with the media sounds glamorous and exciting, it was actually quite distracting. As media attention mounted, so did my level of stress. I began to struggle with my hitting. Last season's smooth, powerful stoke disappeared. I began tinkering with my stance, trying open stances, closed stances, narrow and wide stances. I took extra batting practice every day and used different bat models in an effort to find my stroke.

In the middle of March, *Sports Illustrated* wanted to do a feature article about the new and improved Kansas City Royals, using two other rookies and me. The thought of such an interview made me even more nervous, especially since I hadn't even played a game above the Double-A level. I tried to assure myself I would not say anything that my teammates could find as cocky or arrogant. I continued to struggle at the plate, but the people from *Sports Illustrated* remained adamant about me participating in the upcoming article. I reluctantly agreed to the interview, but it was clear to me that I needed to focus more on what was happening between the white lines.

On the day of the interview, dozens of pictures were taken in the outfield grass at our spring training facility in Fort Myers, Florida. I answered the reporter's questions with safe answers, hoping not to draw the ire of the veteran players on the team. The article appeared on March 20, 1984. Three days later, I was dispatched to the minor leagues for reassignment.

Manager Dick Howser's decision to send me to the minors came as no surprise. My performance in the exhibition games had been miserable. But as disappointed as I was with my performance, I was relieved to land on the Triple-A Omaha team. I figured I would be better off playing everyday in the minors so by the time I made it to the "show," all my problems would be worked out. On April 4th, our team flew from Sarasota, Florida, to Omaha, Nebraska, where we would begin the season as a member of the American Association.

Temperatures that barely exceeded 35 degrees at game time suddenly replaced the heat and humidity of Florida. The climate made it difficult for players to get loose and stay focused. My performance began as frigid as the winds sweeping across the midwestern plains. I managed just three hits in my first 30 plate appearances. Swinging at pitches out of the strike zone earned me 15 strikeouts during that period.

I soon realized that I wasn't getting the same pitches I had seen in previous seasons. The pitching in this league was of a much higher caliber. Whenever I got in a favorable hitting count, I could no longer count on receiving the "room service" fastball that I often feasted on. Instead, I was fed a steady diet of breaking balls, and the more I swung at them, the uglier I looked. Most pitchers in the Association were older, more experienced, and more capable of exposing a batter's weakness.

Through the month of April, my batting average was a paltry .125 with only three RBI in my first 80 at-bats. I felt like a kid playing in a grown-up league. For the first time in my professional career I began to doubt my ability to play at this level. Negative thoughts rolled through my head, such as: "You stink" and "You can't hit anymore." My confidence tumbled to an all-time low. By the All-Star break I had accumulated 200 at-bats while yielding only one home run, 12 RBI, and a career-low batting average of .190—five points lower than my body weight. The Royals' management had been very patient with me—playing me every day despite my struggles—but I wondered how long they would keep me in Triple-A. Thoughts of being demoted to Double-A Jacksonville haunted me. I was desperate. I had to make some kind of adjustment. But I'd been making adjustments all along—subtle changes in hand position or a new position in the batter's box. Nothing worked.

During the All-Star break, I took some time and thought about my relationship to the game. I realized that baseball was no longer fun. It had become a numbers' game, a job, something to do every day—not the kind of attitude a young player could use to achieve peak performance in his third year of pro ball. I realized that I needed a serious

17

attitude adjustment—and quick. Then and there I decided to simply stop following my statistics.

That's right, I gave up the daily need to keep score on myself, to know my batting average or how many RBI and home runs I was accumulating. I even gave up reading newspapers so I wouldn't read what the Omaha sports page might say about me. For this sports junkie, giving up the sports page actually was not a simple thing to do. But I was committed to the experiment—committed to not looking at my statistics for the remainder of the season.

Omaha Royals, 1984. (Photo by Rich Morris)

In early July, I began playing better. Manager Gene Lamont inserted me in the leadoff spot, hoping to boost my confidence. It worked. I began a 14-game hitting streak, spraying line drives to all parts of the field. Pitchers tried pounding me with inside fastballs, but I reacted well to each pitch, regularly pulling the ball down the right-field line. If pitchers stayed away, I waited long enough to drive it to the opposite field. During the first two weeks after my attitude adjustment, I amassed 25 hits and five home runs. Things continued to get better as I kept up the pace through the remainder of July. Baseball was fun again—just the way it was when I was an eight-year-old Little Leaguer. I was on top of my game and I felt unstoppable.

Then came August.

August is the final month of minor league play and our team entered it mired in last place—our ranks decimated by injuries and call-ups to the major league team. We struggled to win only a handful of games. But even with the team struggling, I'd begun the month hitting safely in 12 of the first 15 games.

With two weeks remaining in the season, a doubleheader in Omaha provided a valuable lesson in humility and patience. I perceived these two games as a microcosm of how the entire season had gone for me. Playing against the Louisville Redbirds, we were scheduled to face two of the better pitchers in the league. In the first game, it was a tough left-handed pitcher, Ken Dayley. Short, yet powerful in stature, Dayley possessed an intimidating fastball along with an impressive overhand curveball. He wore his hat low and tight over his eyes in an attempt to unnerve his opponents. The St. Louis Cardinals had sent Dayley to Louisville to polish his already impressive repertoire. I knew facing him for the first time would be a great challenge for the whole team—myself included.

Dayley immediately lived up to his advance billing. Overpowering us in the first three innings, he struck out six of the first nine batters he faced and kept us hitless through the first five frames. My plate appearances against him brought back some painful memories from earlier in the season. Dayley dazzled me with six fastballs. I swung mightily at each one without making contact once. The domination continued during my third at bat; this time Dayley embarrassed me with three consecutive curveballs. Once again, I didn't connect. Six innings and already I was wearing the *sombrero* (three strikeouts in one game).

Our team staged a rally in the ninth, managing to load the bases. But we still trailed, 3-0. I stepped up to the plate with two outs and the bases loaded. This would be my chance to pay back Dayley for all the embarrassment he caused me earlier in the game. Still throwing in the high 80s, Dayley started me off with a belt-high fastball that I swung at and missed. It was a mistake pitch—one that I should have launched into the lion's exhibit at the Omaha Zoo, just beyond the right-field fence. Dayley's next pitch was the nastiest curveball I had ever seen. It caught the outside corner of the plate, and I felt my knees buckle. I was rattled, my newly rebuilt confidence gone. I believed I would've had better luck hitting a butterfly with a shovel.

As I tried to compose myself, I glanced at catcher Tom Nieto. He was doing a poor job of containing his amusement.

"Hey, Nieto," I said, "you think this crap is funny?"

Nieto stood up, his expression difficult to read through his facemask. "Sorry," he said. "Didn't mean to piss you off, but it looks like Dayley has saved his nastiest stuff just for you."

I stepped back into the batter's box muttering some words for Mr. Nieto and Mr. Dayley.

Dayley unloaded his best heater. My eyes tracked the chest-high fastball as it came toward the middle of the plate. Unleashing my most powerful and aggressive stroke, I swung—and missed, striking out to end the game. I now had a set of goat horns to go along with my golden sombrero—striking out four times in one game. Never before in my career had I been so dominated and overmatched. Trying to hide my embarrassment, I hung my head as I walked to the clubhouse, stinging from the boos coming from our normally reserved crowd.

The game was over and I had only 20 minutes to prepare for the second game. I sat in front of my locker feeling humiliated and full of self-pity. After a few minutes I turned to teammate Dave Leeper sitting at my right.

"Hey, Leep," I asked, "you see anything wrong with my swing?"

Leeper let out a laugh. "Johnny Mo," he said, "there are only a handful of guys who could've hit Dayley tonight. And the last time I checked both Ty Cobb and Babe Ruth were dead."

It took a few moments but I finally realized that Leeper was right: there was nothing wrong with my swing. I had just come up against a superior pitcher. Instead of deriding my performance or trying to fix something, I quietly acknowledged Ken Dayley for his outstanding pitching and put the game behind me. In a few minutes I would have another opportunity against Louisville's best right-handed fireballer—a hard-throwing hurler named Kurt Kepshire.

Playing center field and leading off again, my main focus was simply to make contact with the ball. In my first plate appearance, I managed to hit a high fly to center field for an easy out. In the third inning, I reached base on a walk. I came to bat again in the sixth inning with the bases loaded and our team trailing by the score of 3-1. Kepshire challenged me with his best fastball and I popped up the first pitch for the third out of the inning. Flipping my bat in the air, I cursed myself out as I departed the field.

While retrieving my glove from the dugout, I got some coaching from a drunken fan. "Hey, Morris," he shouted, his words somewhat slurred, "you're the biggest rally killer I've ever seen. How many more guys you gonna leave on base?" My immediate instinct was to leap into the stands and wrap my Louisville Slugger around the guy's throat. The last thing I needed was a self-styled pro telling me how lousy I was playing. I already knew.

I came to the plate in the bottom of the eighth with our team trailing, 3-2, with one man on first. I stepped into the batter's box and flashbacks of my failure against Ken Dayley flooded my head. My hecklers

21

had grown to about two dozen sitting right behind homeplate. "Morris, you couldn't hit the broad side of a bull with a steam shovel" and "I've seen better swings on a gate" were some of the more clever rags. Ignoring the noise, I shook myself, took a deep breath, and told myself to stay aggressive.

Omaha Royals, 1984. (Photo by Rich Morris)

After Kepshire's first three pitches, the count stood at two balls and one strike. I readied myself for a fastball on the next delivery, determined not to get beat again. But Kepshire surprised me with a breaking ball up in the strike zone. I unloaded with the most viscous hack I could muster. The bat shuddered as the ball and bat made contact. I started my run to first, watching as the ball disappeared over the light tower behind the right-field wall. I floated around the bases and a feeling of pure ecstasy replaced all the disappointments of the day. My home run put us in the lead and we held on to win by a score of 4-3.

A handful of games remained in the season after that game-winning home run and I finished them on a high note. But in keeping with my promise, I didn't look at my offensive statistics until after the last game. When I finally looked, my credentials were much better than I had anticipated. I'd racked up 15 home runs, 60 RBI, and a batting average of .270. Not bad for a kid who was in real jeopardy of being sent down to Double-A in the middle of the season.

Until the 1984 season in Omaha, I'd gotten used to having my pro career turn out my way. So far, I'd written a pretty good script: first round draft choice, immediate success my first year in Class A, and Southern League MVP honors. Not until Omaha did I experience a prolonged period of failure. Lucky for me, though, those days in Omaha taught me the lesson of a lifetime: sometimes it's better to stop keeping score and to stay in the game.

"Most players from the United States are bothered by the language. We don't know exactly what's being said to us. We complain about the food and living accommodations. It's no wonder the locals look at us "gringos" as ugly, spoiled Americans."

— *Nelson Simmons*

Bottom of the First

GOD BLESS AMERICA

WINTER BALL. THE THOUGHT of spending the off-season away from U.S. soil has a way of either inspiring or intimidating professional baseball players. Some minor leaguers view it as the last piece of the puzzle that will catapult them to major league stardom, while others break out into a cold sweat at the mere mention of three more months of baseball.

My minor league season in Omaha, Nebraska, had just finished in early September of 1984. It had been my first season in Triple-A and I ended the season with a bang, finishing the campaign as the top-rated prospect in the entire Kansas City Royals' organization.

I was back home in New York when the phone rang. It was Dick Balderson, farm director for the Royals. "John, congratulations on your great season. You really finished up strong!"

Balderson's compliment made me feel appreciated. "Thanks, I'm excited about the way the season turned out. I really feel I'm ready for the big leagues. I'll do whatever it takes to make the big league team next season."

My words must have been sweet music to Balderson's ears. "Well John, it's funny you should say that because I'd like you to play winter ball starting next month in the Dominican Republic."

My interest was piqued. "You'll play for the Escogido team, which plays in the capital city of Santo Domingo. Your salary will be $5,000 a month. More importantly, the experience will help accelerate your progress to the major leagues."

That was all I needed to hear. Sign me up and let's go. I was all for anything that would get me to "the show." At the same time, I faintly remembered some ominous things I'd heard about winter ball with its tough competition and larger, more hostile crowds.

I flew into Santo Domingo on the 15th of October. I clambered down from the small turbo-prop plane and walked across the tarmac towards the terminal. All of a sudden, I felt like a lost child on his first day of school—out of my comfort zone and scared to death. The temperature had swelled to 100 degrees and my eyes burned as I squinted up at the sun. Spanish-speaking airport agents barked out rapid-fire instructions to anyone within listening distance. Atop the terminal building was a small battalion of soldiers dressed in battle fatigues. Machine guns, rifles, and grenades were all within reach, and they appeared ready to use them if any trouble arose. Until then, the largest contingent of soldiers I'd ever seen on Long Island had been the Color Guard at an Islanders' hockey game, so I worried that I was walking into the most dangerous country in the world.

After retrieving my bags I hailed a cab for the 15-minute ride to the hotel—my home for the next three months. We sped along the bumpy roads past homes that looked hopelessly thrown together, hastily constructed tin shacks held together with tires, cinder blocks, and rope. Sewage and garbage puddled along the roadside creating a terrible stench.

While I bounced in my seat holding on for dear life, I watched the locals work their way around the city streets. Their clothing was dirty, ripped, and old. Children bathed themselves in rivulets of filthy water.

Little kids walked around barefoot. All kinds of animals clogged the streets. Dogs, cats, goats, cows, chickens, and horses shared the city with the rest of the population. They all looked sick—their skeletal features gave every indication that it had been a while since their last meal and bath.

By the end of the first day, the heat, humidity, and foul odor in the air had robbed me of both appetite and energy. I settled into my hotel room that evening and by the next day it was time to play ball.

Our first game was against our cross-town rivals, the Licey Lions. I played right field that evening and batted fifth. I led off the second inning, swinging through three high fastballs against my Dominican adversary. Two innings later I struck out again, swinging through three high fastballs. I returned to the outfield amid a chorus of boos from the hometown fans. A batting helmet would have come in handy, as batteries, coins, and rocks rained down upon me. A simple message was being sent—my Dominican honeymoon was over.

My next two plate appearances produced weak groundballs to the second baseman. The hometown faithful continued their target practice. Objects buzzed by my head for the remainder of the game. If this was the treatment I was going to get from the home fans, I couldn't wait to see what awaited me on the first road trip. Although I figured it couldn't get much worse than this. Or could it?

One game down and only 59 to go.

Time came to a standstill during the first handful of games. After the first week, our team won one of six games. My batting average was an abysmal .150, and with only one extra basehit to my credit, it felt like I was using a rolled up newspaper for a bat. But the following week our team won five in a row. I began hitting the ball with some authority and it felt good to be a part of the team's success. Then during that fateful third week, my fortunes turned quickly. Suddenly, I found myself confronted with a series of events that would test my physical and psychological well-being.

One overcast morning in mid-November, I walked to a nearby

shopping mall with my roommate Nelson Simmons. Nelson was a top-rated outfield prospect in the Detroit Tigers' organization. He was in peak condition, standing 5' 10" and weighing a chiseled 235 pounds. His thick torso bulged with muscles and his biceps felt like granite. He could have easily passed as a Mike Tyson body double. Though he was a friendly guy, Nelson looked intimidating and I knew that no one would mess around with him. I actually felt safe walking the streets with him. It was great having a bodyguard who was also a nice guy.

While at the mall, we browsed through stores for several hours, killing time before getting back to the hotel. As we stepped outside, a torrential downpour greeted us. So instead of walking the six blocks back to the hotel we grabbed a cab. The two-minute ride was worth the four pesos we paid to the elderly taxi driver. At least we stayed dry.

After changing our clothes we headed downstairs to the lobby. As we approached the main entrance, a loud commotion near the reception desk startled us. Manny, the hotel manager, was shouting at an elderly man—the same man who minutes earlier had given us our ride to the hotel.

As he noticed us, he wagged his finger at us, shouting at Manny in Spanish.

"What seems to be the problem, Manny?" I asked upon reaching the desk. Manny looked at us suspiciously before responding. "The driver say you no pay him enough pesos for ride to hotel. He say you each owe five more pesos." Manny's face tightened and his voice quivered. He wanted no part of this mess.

The driver continued his tirade in the background while I tried to speak over his hysterical voice. "When I gave the driver his money, he had no problem with us. He seemed grateful that we gave him such a generous tip."

Over the next few minutes, Manny served as referee between the taxi driver and me. Eventually, the boxing gloves came off—verbal jabs careened around the lobby as four-letter words in both languages filled the air. The insanity continued for another five minutes before Nelson

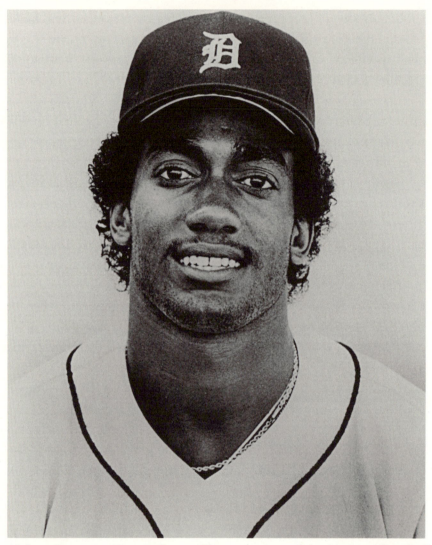

Nelson Simmons, Detroit Tigers. (Photo courtesy of the National Baseball Hall of Fame Library, Cooperstown, NY)

stepped forward. Underneath his quiet disposition, a hot temper was beginning to boil.

As Nelson tried to restore order, a policeman nonchalantly entered the lobby. He was dressed in a dark gray uniform and black boots. Sunglasses hid his eyes and a three-inch long scar ran down his left cheek. His expression was blank. The revolver in his holster was in full view for all to see and my legs weakened at the sight of it. Then my throat tightened and my mouth went dry. Something was wrong. Dead wrong.

Manny turned his attention towards me again, his look spelling trouble. "The driver say that in the last 20 minutes, he lose *mucho dinèro* arguing with you about the ride. So now you each owe him *10 more pesos*." In a flash, I realized we were being set up by a team of ruthless characters bent on taking the rich "gringos" for another ride. And there wasn't a damn thing we could do about it.

Nelson was beginning to show further signs of losing his composure. He pounded his fists and gritted his teeth—then directed his wrath at the driver, "Take a hike, old man. I don't have time to deal with this crap."

Meanwhile the officer loitered by quietly—watching and waiting. Finally he stepped forward and made his move. He took off his glasses and revealed a cold dark stare. He looked at me sternly before speaking in Spanish.

I didn't need Manny's translation to realize we were in trouble. Manny cleared his throat before beginning the translation. "Gentlemen, the officer say you have one minute to pay the driver his *20 pesos*. If you no pay him, he arrest you, put you in police car, and take you to sugar cane field to work for the rest of the day."

My hand flew into my pocket, fumbling to find my wallet. Within seconds I produced 20 pesos and tossed it at the driver in disgust.

Scooping it up, the cop and the driver vanished. Nelson and I were left standing in the lobby. We had been set up—targeted by two outlaws, and there wasn't anything we could do about it.

Chapter two began several days after the incident. I attended a Thanksgiving Day dinner that was thrown together by the owners of the team. The entire organization was invited to the first-class affair. The team owners seemed especially interested in accommodating the American players because most of them were away from their families and they spared no expense on the celebration. There was live music, great food, an open bar, and an outdoor setting at the most exclusive country club in the Dominican Republic, which had the most breath-taking view of the ocean and the city. The dinner was an awesome display of entrees—including turkey, ham, and pork. But, by the end of the night, I had become violently ill. What started out as minor stomach cramps turned into violent episodes of vomiting which lasted into the morning.

For the next week I was quarantined in my hotel room and I quickly dropped 15 pounds. A doctor told me I had trichinosis—some fancy medical term for food poisoning I was informed later. In any case, it left me lethargic, listless, and unmotivated. How in the world was I ever going to be able to play ball in this condition? I was becoming the proverbial 98-pound weakling who spends most of the day on the beach having sand kicked in his face.

Ten days after getting sick, I returned to the team. My once custom-fit uniform hung loosely on me. When I walked into the mosquito infected clubhouse, manager Felipe Alou greeted me and commented on my appearance. "Hey Johnny, it looks like you've missed a few meals." My arms and legs looked like pencils, atrophied from weight loss and inactivity. My face was pale and drawn. Felipe was right. I looked awful.

I spent the next few days running sprints and hitting in the batting cage in an effort to get back into playing shape. The task became much more difficult than I originally imagined. The bat felt like a log. My legs felt like 10-pound weights hung from each of them. Even so, after just three days of training, I made the mistake of informing Alou that I was ready to play. What an idiot! Who the hell was I trying to impress?

Alou wasted no time inserting my name into the lineup. And just as quickly I stunk up the joint. That night I struck out my first three at-bats. I was overmatched the next two games as well. By the end of the week, I had gone 15 at-bats without a hit, including 10 strikeouts—not exactly the stuff that legends are made of. There appeared to be no relief in sight as far as I was concerned.

The thought of quitting and going home to New York began to creep into my mind. I wanted to get the hell out of town and regroup. I was at the end of my rope and leaving seemed like it might be the best thing to do.

On the 1st of December we received our paychecks in the morning. After cashing the check, it was time to head to the ballpark for the rest of the day. That evening we played an extra-inning game, losing in the 12th by a score of 6-4. The marathon affair took us past midnight and it was 2 A.M. before I returned to the hotel.

Wearily, I trudged into my room. Something was wrong. Within seconds it hit me. The furniture had been moved. The dresser drawers and my closets were out of place. My suitcases, briefcase, and clothes where not in the same place I had left them. Sweat poured down my face as I tore apart the rooms searching for my valuables. My portable tape player was missing, along with $3,000 in cold hard cash.

This was the last straw. As far as I was concerned, it was time to get the hell out of this God-forsaken hole.

The following afternoon I stormed into Felipe Alou's office ready to do battle. I ranted for 20 minutes about all the incidents that had taken place since my arrival. I raged about the taxi cab fiasco, the food poisoning, my abysmal baseball performance, and now the mystery surrounding my stolen money.

"So Felipe, considering everything that's happened to me over the past six weeks, I want my release. This has been a nightmare. I want out."

I sat and waited for his answer. Felipe stared at me for several seconds before responding. "I'm sorry you've had such a tough time. I'm not gonna argue with you. You can have your release."

Thank God! There it was, short and sweet and no argument. I was going home. I was somewhat surprised Felipe didn't offer a bit more resistance, but maybe since Felipe was a Dominican native and veteran winter ball manger, he had probably seen other American players struggle as well. I was now free to return to the comfortable surroundings of the United States. Over the next 48 hours I filled out immigration papers, cleared out my apartment, said "adios" to my now former

teammates, and silently wondered if I'd made a serious mistake by asking for my release. Maybe I should have kept my mouth shut and played
out the remaining five weeks of the season. Would the Royals' organization be disappointed in me for not showing a stronger resolve? What
would my friends and family back home think of me? But it didn't seem
to matter. I realized that spring training was not too far away, and I
would need this extra time to get both my body and mind in shape.

Days later, on December 5th I landed at New York's JFK Airport. I
hopped off the plane excited that I'd soon see my mom. As I approached
the baggage claim area, I could see her off in the distance. Right there
I stopped, dropped my two carry-on bags to the ground, and fell to
my knees.

I bent over, lowered my head, and kissed the ground. Never before
in my life was I so thankful for living in the United States. I looked up
and whispered the first words that came to mind. "God Bless America!"

Minutes later the two of us were off to Long Island. Back to the
split-levels, backyard pools, and friendly neighborhoods of Long Island.

Maybe Mom was right. There really is no place like home!

"Maybe being a minor league baseball player makes you insane. Maybe you just have to be crazy to be a minor league baseball player."

—Jim Bouton

Top of the Second

WAKE-UP CALL

THE TELEPHONE WAS RINGING as I entered my apartment in Omaha. Dropping my golf bag just inside the door, I managed to field the receiver on the fifth ring. Little did I know that this particular phone call would forever alter my perception of the game I love, or that the three most uncomfortable days of my professional baseball career were about to begin.

It was the middle of May 1985, and things were going well. With three years of minor league experience under my belt and my second season in the Cornhusker State off to a good start, I figured a call to the parent club was not too far away.

"Good morning, Johnny," said my mom. It was great hearing her voice on the other end of the phone line, but I wondered why she would call me at 10 A.M. "I've been waiting for you to call," she continued. "When were you planning on telling us the big news?"

I was lost. Not knowing what she was talking about, I dove into a boring replay of my early morning heroics on the links. "Well, Mom, let's see, I shot an 82 this morning. Kept the ball in the fairway. I three-putted a few times, but overall I played well."

"Johnny," she fired back, "I could care less about golf right now. I want to know when you were going to let us know you've been traded!"

My jaw dropped and my knees weakened, as if someone had landed a punch. I cleared my throat and said, "Mom, I haven't been traded. I played a good game last night, but nobody said anything about a trade."

I could hear the sound of shuffling papers coming through the phone. "It's right here in the *New York Daily News*," she said. "You've been traded to the St. Louis Cardinals for Lonnie Smith."

A cold wave passed through my body and I felt lightheaded. The collar of my golf shirt felt tighter around my neck. Standing alone in my apartment, I wondered if I was somehow caught in the midst of a bad dream.

Forcing myself to snap out of it, I said, "The Royals wouldn't trade me, Mom. It's gotta be a mistake. I'll make a few phone calls and find out what the hell is going on." I hurried my mom off the line, leaving her as confused as I was.

I immediately placed a call to my manager, Gene Lamont. Gene had been my manager for the previous two seasons and I considered him to be an honest man. Certainly he would tell me the truth about any such ridiculous rumors. I reached Gene, but he sounded as confused as I was. "Johnny Mo," he started, "I have no idea what you're talking about. Just come to the park later and stop worrying. Everything is fine." I hung up and stared into space. Gene had sounded convincing, but I still wasn't sure. After all, how could a trade be announced in the newspapers without my manager knowing about it?

Feeling the need for a second opinion, I picked up the phone and called the front office in Kansas City. Dick Balderson, our farm director, was the first person I reached, but he had little to say on any impending trade. "You have nothing to worry about John. You'll be playing center field tonight, just like you have since the season began." I heard the words, but something I couldn't put my finger on seemed out of whack.

My antennae were up now. I wanted an answer and I wanted it *now!* My next call was to John Schurholz, general manager of the Royals. He answered the phone on the first ring. After a few pleasantries I asked him about the rumors. "Johnny," he said, "the news about you being traded is strictly a rumor created by the St. Louis media. You have nothing to worry about. Everything will be fine."

I'd now heard from three prominent people in the Royals' organization. Each had confirmed that I was staying put. I now believed that the article Mom read in the newspaper was either a misprint, or a rumor spread by a sportswriter eager to make a name for himself.

Reassured, I went to the park that afternoon knowing that I was still a member of the Omaha Royals. Upon entering the clubhouse, I checked the lineup card that hung on the entry door, just like I did every day. Strangely, my name was missing. In the three seasons I'd been playing for the Royals, rarely had I ever received an off day. Besides, Balderson had told me earlier in the day that I'd be in the starting lineup. What, I wondered, could have happened?

My manager approached me at my locker as I was dressing. I detected a tightness in his face and his eyes wandered as he began to speak. His voice was low and subdued. "I'm going to sit you down tonight," he said. "You've been playing every day and you need a break."

I heard Lamont's words, but sensed that something was left unsaid.

That night, I sat out the entire game in the dugout, thinking dark thoughts. Had the Royals brass lied to me earlier in the day? Could this be the start of an ugly series of events that was quickly going to get worse? But then, maybe Lamont was right. Maybe I did need a day off. But why had he acted so strangely?

Hearing nothing more that night or the following morning, I strode into the clubhouse the next afternoon, sure that my name would be in the starting lineup. However, the once easy task of checking the batting order—one that I took for granted each and every day—now had an almost desperate twist to it. My name was missing from the lineup for the second consecutive day. That did it. I was determined to get to the bottom of it.

The veins in my neck bulged as I marched towards Lamont's office. He displayed an air of extreme discomfort as I barged into his space. "Gene," I asked, "what's going on here? This is the second day in a row I'm not playing."

He fidgeted in his swivel chair for a second before replying. Clearly avoiding eye contact, he quietly responded, "They're starting a tough lefty who has given you trouble in the past, so I'm giving you another night off."

It was a line of garbage, and we both knew it. "Are you kidding me? I've played the past two years for you and you've never given me a day off, not to mention two days off in a row! Just tell me the damn truth."

Like a little boy caught with his hand in a cookie jar, Gene's defense cracked a little, but not completely. "OK, John, something is in the works. But I'm not allowed to say anything about it right now. You'll come on the road trip with us tomorrow and we'll have more information when we arrive in Buffalo. In the meantime I'm asking you to be patient for one more day."

I left the skipper's office in a daze. Gene had confirmed my worst fears—that I'd been lied to from the head office on down. That night I sought refuge in the far corner of the training room—far away from teammates, coaches, the media, and the game I so loved. I wanted to be left alone, to wallow in my personal stew of anger and self-pity.

The following morning, our team departed for Buffalo. Sitting alone in the airport terminal, I remained withdrawn from my teammates. Confusion and sadness overwhelmed me as I searched for an answer that made sense. Had I screwed up somehow? Did I do something to piss somebody off? Could it be that the Royals thought I wasn't good enough to make it in the big leagues?

The flight gave me too much time to anticipate the terrible news that certainly lay ahead of me in Buffalo. I felt like a young man awaiting sentencing, yet not even knowing what terrible crime had been committed.

Upon reaching my hotel room, I saw the red message light on my telephone flashing. The front desk informed me that I had a message from John Schurholz in Kansas City. I was to call him immediately. I dialed the phone and sensed that bad news was only minutes away. My throat tightened and my hands began to shake. John answered the phone and I had to swallow hard before speaking. "John Schurholz, this is John Morris. I'm returning your phone call."

"John," he started, "we just made a trade. You've been dealt to the St. Louis Cardinals for Lonnie Smith. I know we discussed this the other day, but at the time I couldn't give you any information."

A sudden wave of relief flooded through my body. The suspense was finally over. The next instant, though, the relief was replaced by anger. A nasty smirk formed on my face as I recalled our conversation only three days earlier. John had been the one who had suggested that my trade to the Cardinals was strictly a rumor. Feeling somewhat liberated now that I had a new employer, I said, "So, you knew all along that I

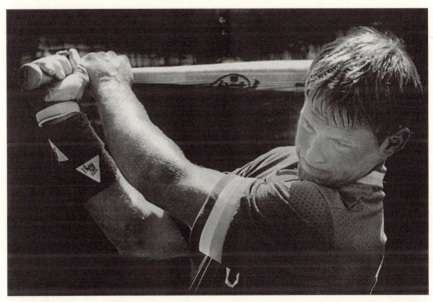

Spring training, 1985, Fort Myers, FL. (Photo credit: Keith Myers/The Kansas City Star)

was going to be traded. I think it's unfortunate that I had to find out from my mom who just happened to stumble upon it in the newspaper."

"Listen, John," he said, "you're going to a first-class organization and we know you will do well with the Cardinals. Right now we need a veteran major leaguer so that's why we traded for Lonnie Smith. Whitey Herzog is a great manager who thinks the world of you. He even told me that himself in spring training. I want to wish you luck and hope everything goes well for the rest of your career."

End of conversation. Have a nice day; it was nice knowing you.

A wake-up call had been issued compliments of the Kansas City Royals. Perhaps my disappointment and frustration stemmed from knowing I'd never make it to the majors with the team that originally drafted me. Or maybe I was living in a fantasyland—hoping I'd play my entire career with one organization—just like George Brett had done with the Royals. Or maybe the thought of reading an article from *The Sporting News* troubled me—when Dick Balderson, just prior to spring training was quoted as saying, "John Morris will be a fixture in Kansas City for many years to come."

I hung up the phone with my first unpleasant taste of the game I'd grown up with. No longer just a game, I now saw baseball was a big business, and, as such, sometimes decisions were made and carried out with little regard for those involved. I suppose that learning this was part of growing up.

Later that afternoon I met my sister Joan for lunch. She had driven all the way from Vermont to see me play for the first time in years. Instead, she became the first member of my family to receive the official news of the trade. I said good-bye to my now former teammates. I felt sad, knowing that I was leaving a group of guys I loved playing with— guys such as Dave Leeper, Tony Ferreira, Bill Pecota, and David Cone. We had risen through the ranks together—riding the same team buses, eating in the same dumpy restaurants, and staying in the same two-star hotels. I never enjoy saying farewell under any circumstances, but this time it was particularly painful.

After the evening flight back to Omaha, I was too busy to think much about the trade. But cruising the long stretches of interstate toward Louisville, Kentucky, over the next two days gave me plenty of time to reflect on my career in the Royals' organization. As the miles flashed by, the bitterness and anger that I had developed towards the Royals began to fade. After all, soon I was headed for the home of the Redbirds—my new team. And that meant new opportunities awaited me. It was time to move ahead. Soon enough, I would find out that this trade opened the door to my major league dream.

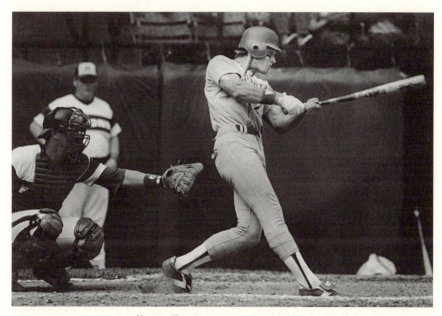

My new team, Louisville Redbirds, 1985. Grandslam in Buffalo, NY. (Photo by Rich Morris)

"I don't know how Abner Doubleday would have felt about the game, but Laurel and Hardy would have loved it."

—Harvey Aronson

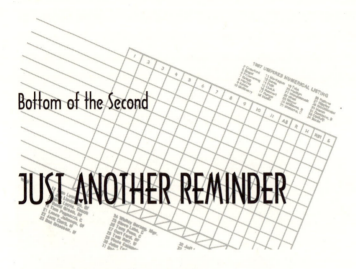

Bottom of the Second

JUST ANOTHER REMINDER

I LOVED COLLEGE BASEBALL for its thrills, atmosphere, and excitement. But I never got excited about the marathon bus rides from New Jersey to places like Chapel Hill, North Carolina, and Miami, Florida. As a matter of fact, I hated them and when it came to food, eating too often at Wendy's and Burger King left a lousy taste in my mouth while lodging at places with names like "The Dew Drop Inn" rarely ever provided a decent night's sleep. I was certain, as I left the collegiate scene in June '82, that life as a "pro" would see me, if not immediately in it, at least near the lap of luxury.

But a year and a half later, after "beating the bushes" in the Florida State League (Class-A) and the Southern League (Double-A) I realized that minor league travel bore a striking resemblance to what I had endured in my college days.

The low minors were not without some subtle improvements when it came to life on the road. Bus trips rarely ever exceeded 14 hours, and a wave of aluminum beer cans rolling towards the back of the bus (while we churned up some hill in Alabama) often served as an alarm clock as we struggled to wake up. Instead of having to choose between Kentucky Fried Chicken, Taco Bell, and Steak and Shake, we'd sometimes visit a truck stop for a bite to eat. I always enjoyed watching teammates fight over who'd get the last piece of dried-out chicken that had spent the last three hours under a heat lamp. For us on a strict budget, the truck stop was the ideal place to buy a loaf of bread and a jar of peanut butter and jelly.

Once our team found our evening's rest at the "White House." Unfortunately, this half-star hotel lacked all the amenities that our leaders in the nation's capital receive each and every day. But I vowed not to complain too much. After all, I was playing professional baseball and I was not about to let a few inconveniences stand in the way of my getting to the big leagues.

After I was promoted to Triple-A I was sure that life would become a whole lot easier. Airplanes replaced buses and the additional $10 we received each day in meal allowance surely came in handy. But while Triple-A life was only one step from "the show," it was still a far cry from the pampered lifestyle of a major leaguer.

One particular road trip in the summer of 1985 demonstrated just how far it was. Our Louisville Redbirds went on the road to Buffalo for a four-game series. We met at the airport at 5 A.M., and by 6 A.M. we were flying the friendly skies. First, we flew west to St. Louis, where we'd catch the first of our two connecting flights. An hour after landing we were back in the air on our way to Pittsburgh. From there, after a 45-minute delay due to inclement weather we boarded our last flight and headed to upstate New York. We landed an hour late, but in the minor leagues that isn't all too uncommon. Our team staggered off the airplane, hobbled down to the baggage claim area, retrieved our bags, and hopped on a bus for the Holiday Inn in downtown Buffalo. Although we were pressed for time, the plan was to check into our rooms, grab a bite to eat, then head to War Memorial Stadium for the 7 o'clock game against the Buffalo Bisons.

Half an hour after the old beat up Greyhound bus grinded its way out of the airport, the Redbirds poured into the hotel lobby. The lady at the front desk appeared nervous as we approached her. "You guys aren't the Louisville baseball team, are you?" she asked. Our travel-wearied skipper, Jim Fregosi, barked, "Yes, and we'd like to check into our rooms." The young lady shrunk behind the desk and cleared her throat. "I'm sorry guys, but your rooms won't be ready for a few more hours. You can check in after the game tonight."

Still hanging onto a semblance of civility, Tom Pagnozzi chimed in, "Well, then tell us where the hotel restaurant is so we can get something to eat."

"Just around the corner at the end of the hallway," she said.

Twelve of us stormed off towards the restaurant. As we closed the distance to within 10 feet of the doorway a piece of paper taped to the window came into view. We came closer. A dozen pair of eyes fixed on the note. The message provided us with more information then we wanted about the facility we were staying in:

The New York State Board of Health has temporarily shut down our restaurant. We apologize for any inconvenience. There is a Denny's and a McDonalds around the corner in case you're interested.

"This place is a dump," moaned pitcher Greg Mathews. "Now what are we gonna do?"

Time was becoming an issue and Fregosi came up with an idea that made sense. "All right guys, on the bus in 10 minutes. It's only a five-minute ride to the park. When we get there, we'll order some pizza before the game."

So away we went through the city streets of Buffalo. But optimism soon turned to concern. It appeared that our bus driver, right out of driving school, was unfamiliar with the Buffalo area and the where-abouts of the 65,000-seat War Memorial Stadium. He seemed a bit confused as he scratched his head at every intersection. Our suspicions grew as we watched the barely visible tops of the stadium lights shrink towards the horizon and finally disappear from our view.

Jack Ayer unloaded from the backseat. "Hey bussy, don't you know where the hell you're going?" The driver ignored the outburst. He was determined to make up for his blunder. Suddenly, pulling a hard right down a side street in an effort to right his wrong only compounded his error. Over the next 25 minutes we were greeted by a maze of detours, one-way streets, and dead ends. Joe Magrane shook his head from across the aisle, and perhaps still heady from his famous crack concerning the whereabouts of JFK ("Do you mean the President or the airport?") yelled out to nobody in particular: "Buffalo is gonna be a great city some day as soon as they get done with it."

It was almost 6 o'clock when the bus wheezed into the parking lot of the stadium. By now, the thought of throwing down some hot food before the game was out of the question. It was time to drag our tired bodies up to the cramped visitors' clubhouse.

Another surprise was waiting for us.

The clubhouse was surprisingly uncluttered when we walked in. It took only a few seconds for us to realize that all of our equipment bags were missing. And nobody had the slightest idea where they were or whether they'd find their way to the stadium. So we sat around for 20 minutes in our street clothes complaining about the plane delays, hotel accommodations, lost equipment, and bus rides we'd encountered that day. Soon we had only 20 minutes before the start of the game. Suddenly a group of teens dressed in Bisons uniforms came into the clubhouse dragging our equipment bags. They rudely dumped them on the floor. By now most of us didn't care where they had been.

After some minutes we filtered down to the field for the start of the game. I took a few seconds to glance around the ancient stadium. It looked very much like the auto racetrack it had been in the 1940s. It was indeed where Robert Redford had poked the pennant winner into the light stanchions in *The Natural* and I realized that this was the field where O.J. Simpson had made his mark in his early gridiron days. I also wondered how many hundreds of minor leaguers over the decades used this field as a springboard to major league stardom.

43

Louisville Redbirds. (Photo by Stan Denny)

Before I knew it I was in the batter's box in the top of the first trying to snap myself out of my fog. But there wouldn't be any magical moments coming from our team on this warm summer night. Instead, we moped around the field like a lifeless band of zombies. We felt and played like crap as the Bisons pounded us into submission.

After the game we feasted on cold pizza, potato chips, and flat Pepsi. Bare asses and elbows, along with a few wet towels, flew past me from every direction. Within a few minutes the showers were out of hot water and a variety of odors suggested a serious plumbing problem. "Just another reminder," belched Billy Lyons from his locker. The first day of this road trip from hell was off to a typical minor league start. The joy of winning two of the next three was dampened by the knowledge that it was time to start thinking about the return trip home.

We all hoped the trip back to Louisville would be less eventful than that of five days ago. True to form, we were back at the airport at 5 A.M. following the last game of the series. After we arrived in Pittsburgh without any problems, we figured, "One flight down with only two to go." Home was just a couple of hours away.

But we spoke too soon.

After boarding the flight in Pittsburgh for St. Louis, we pushed out from the gate and taxied out for several minutes. Then the wait began. For no apparent reason, and with no explanation , we sat motionless on the taxiway for 10 minutes. Finally, a voice chimed in over the intercom. "Ladies and gentlemen, this is your captain speaking. We're experiencing some mechanical problems. Unfortunately, we have to go back to the gate and have a mechanic look at the plane. We'll get back to you on the status of the flight. Thank you for your patience." A collective groan filled the cabin of the DC-9. Some players slumped in their seats while others, perhaps the more fortunate, continued snoring through the news. Upon returning to the gate, the captain turned off the engines. The temperature inside the cabin crept upwards. It didn't take long before passengers were soon bathed in their own sweat and misery. "I'm baking in here," yelled Joe Pettini. "Throw another log on the fire." And we sat. After a half-hour wait the captain came on again. "Um, ladies and gentlemen, the problem with the plane is much worse than what we originally thought. We're going to have to cancel this flight. As you de-plane a gate agent will assist you in helping you find another flight."

We lumbered off the plane. Most of us held our emotions in check. But the frustration of the trip, coupled with this early morning surprise, was more than veteran pitcher Rick Ownby could handle. "All right, that's it. I quit!" screamed the hard-throwing righty as he slammed his rolled-up newspaper to the ground. "This league sucks!" Smartly, we decided to let him steam in a corner.

Minutes later we were back on the concourse. Trainer and traveling secretary "Hap" Hudson huddled with airline employees in an attempt to get us back in the air. "Mr. Hudson, we can get you on the next flight to St. Louis, which leaves here at 2 o'clock. We apologize for any inconvenience." The thought of a three-hour delay did not go over well with the boys, but our frustration was giving way to fatigue as we were looking more and more like the cast of The Night of the Living Dead.

Hours later we finally landed in St. Louis. Naturally, our cancelled flight had caused us to miss our connecting flight to Louisville. But once again "Hap" worked his magic and was able to get us back to Louisville at 6 P.M.—exactly one hour before our game that evening. Twenty-five players and coaches, with bad hair, bad breath, and glazed looks on their mugs, waited around a carousel for their luggage. After another seemingly endless wait, our bags began to appear. All the while the characters in the climatic scene readied themselves in the wings.

Some 20 feet behind us a slightly loud discussion distracted us. An airport security guard stood dressed in dark green pants and a starched white shirt with matching green tie. His "Smokey the Bear" hat and dark glasses hid his expressionless face. Standing before the cop was a 300-pound muscle-bound giant. A heavyweight wearing a long ponytail, mirrored sunglasses, and tattoos on his enormous arms. I knew this giant was not a man to mess with. I began to wonder if maybe the World Wrestling Federation was in town. The cop listened intently. It didn't take long to get to the heart of the matter.

"Officer, I'm the personal body guard for Mr. Andre Agassi, the tennis professional. He's in town for an exhibition. I'm asking for extra security so he can avoid any problems with overzealous fans as we leave the airport." The security guard was not amused by the giant's request. He studied his subject and chose his words carefully. "My friend, I've got one thing to tell ya" he drawled. "I don't know what part of the states y'all are from. But here in blue grass country, unless you're a member of "Hee-Haw," you and your tennis buddy don't have a dang thing to worry about. Now grab your stuff and have a nice day."

We could only burst out laughing. The cop's performance was a thing of beauty. It was the perfect ending to a perfectly insane trip.

The road trip from hell was now in the record books. *Alice in Wonderland* had come face to face with the cast from *One Flew over the Cuckoo's Nest*, and we had been magically transported into that mystical, minor league land known as "The Twilight Zone."

47

"The older they get, the better they were when they were younger."
—Jim Bouton

Top of the Third

"BULLET BOB" COMES TO LOUISVILLE

HE PITCHED FOR THE Cleveland Indians during baseball's Golden Age. Between 1936 and 1956, he dominated American League hitters, accumulating 266 wins and striking out 2,581 batters. His brilliant career landed his name in Baseball's Hall of Fame. His name is Bob Feller and I had the opportunity to meet him during the summer of 1986.

Bob was making a promotional tour of professional baseball parks around the country. At the time, I was playing Triple-A baseball for the Louisville Redbirds—the top minor league affiliate of the St. Louis Cardinals. Bob was in town for the "Night of the Stars"—a weekly feature the marketing department used to pack the stadium during our home games. Each week featured a different Hall-of-Fame guest.

Bob and the marketing department decided to add an interesting feature to his visit. Bob agreed to pitch to a group of local radio disc jockeys as part of an entertaining batting exhibition. The event was set to begin 45 minutes prior to our home game against the Nashville Sounds with the hope of filling the stadium.

My first glimpse of the man came at 3:30 that afternoon. As he dressed in his neatly pressed Cleveland Indians uniform, retired 30 years earlier, I suddenly was thrilled to know that I was sharing the same dressing room with a legend. I walked over and introduced myself. He was upbeat and friendly. The next 30 minutes evolved into a series of stories about the good old days. His eyes brightened and his words quickened when he got to the parts about his dominating fastball.

Then, the subject sadly veered into perilous territory. As the topic changed to the "modern" era, Bob's face twisted and tensed. One nearby player asked his thoughts on how he would have fared against the modern day hitter. Another asked his thoughts on Nolan Ryan, the all-time strikeout leader. Unexpectedly Feller began lashing out at the players, the mere mention of Ryan's name igniting his anger. "The modern day player is spoiled," he said. "Overpaid and overrated as far as I'm concerned." His assault steamrolled in this direction for several more minutes, then he shifted his wrath towards Nolan Ryan. "As far as Ryan is concerned, he couldn't shine my shoes! I was a much better pitcher than him. If he pitched in my era, he would've gotten his butt kicked."

I soon tired of Feller's grousing, and went outside to find a spot for the batting practice exhibition. Feller strode onto the field at 6:30. Glancing around the stands, he appeared annoyed that only a handful of fans had gathered to watch him pitch. The look in his eyes and tightness around his mouth suggested that he would rather be pitching in front of a packed house.

The public address announcer intoned a welcome to one of the greatest pitchers of all time, and Feller trotted out to the pitcher's mound. He threw several warm-up pitches then signaled to his opponents that he was ready to do battle. The rules of the exhibition were that each player would get five swings. The out-of-shape radio personalities looked sadly overmatched even before the first pitch was thrown.

Top of the Third

Bob Feller in his early days. (Photo courtesy of the National Baseball Hall of Fame Library, Cooperstown, NY)

"Bullet Bob's" first pitches made it apparent that he was not going to go easy on the DJs. The first two hitters struggled to make contact; the best they could manage were a few foul balls popped straight up into the batting cage. Feller teased the pseudo-jocks with a variety of pitches, the likes of which they had never seen. Feller may have been 30 years past his prime, but his competitive spirit still raged inside.

Shocking all of us who watched from the dugout, Feller began throwing breaking balls in what could only have been an attempt to further intimidate his overmatched opponents. We could almost sense Feller grasping for the domination he'd enjoyed during his glory years. The next five hitters did little more than dribble an occasional roller past the pitcher's mound. It eventually appeared that Feller was becoming bored with the event. He even became agitated when one or two hitters made the mistake of taking pitches that were close to the strike zone. "Swing the bat, you lazy bum," he barked several times.

But an avenger was only a few feet away down the bench. A veteran of 15 major league seasons and my teammate, Steve Braun, sat beside me in the dugout doing a slow burn as he watched the entire debacle. As each minute passed, Brauns' contempt for Feller grew. Suddenly, Braun jumped to his feet. "I can't watch this crap anymore, I'm gonna put this guy in his place." The tone in his voice suggesting that Bob Feller was about to receive a serious lesson in humility.

Braun headed for the clubhouse. Several minutes later, he reentered the dugout wearing the same clothes he had worn to the park that day. He paused only briefly before quietly walking onto the field, a bat held nonchalantly in his hands. Braun walked to the front of the line of batters, took some practice swings, and waited for his turn.

All the while, Feller continued his mastery of the inferior competition. Finally, another beaten hitter dragged himself out of the cage. Braun stepped into the batter's box and set his feet before glancing up at the aging superstar. "Hey, old man," cried Braun, "throw that tired fastball over the plate so I can see how far I can hit it."

Feller's eyes opened wide at the outrage, incensed that a batter would show such disrespect. Feller went into his windup and delivered his best 1940s fastball belt-high over the inner half of the plate. Braun swung, connected, and the ball sailed over the right-field wall. The next two pitches met with identical results. Braun watched each titanic blast with joy, knowing he was giving Bob Feller a well-deserved comeuppance.

The intensity of the contest escalated as Feller made his intentions perfectly clear. "I'm not done with you yet," he said. "You got lucky. That's the last time you'll make contact."

With teeth clenched and veins bulging from his neck, Feller delivered his next pitch with purpose and conviction. But Braun was equal to the task as his short quick swing sent a viscious line drive shooting past Feller's face. Feller was furious, and became even more determined. He delivered five more pitches to Braun, each resulting in screaming line drives to all areas of the field.

Finally, an angry Feller announced that his next pitch would be his last. But he was determined to make Braun look bad just one time. Feller pounded his glove with his fist before going into his delivery. He had intended to keep the ball low and away, but he made a mistake— a big mistake. Rather than outside, Feller's weary last pitch floated over the middle of the plate. Braun's eyes must have lit up as the fat offering approached homeplate.

Braun hit it right on the screws, crushing the white pearl straight back at Feller. This time Feller was not so fortunate. The ball smashed him squarely on the right shin and ricocheted sharply into the first-base dugout. Feller winced in agony, desperately trying to conceal the pain inflicted by the ball. He stood still and silent on the mound for several seconds. All at once his shoulders drooped and he limped off the field, his sullen expression indicating both frustration and contempt for his adversary.

The pre-game festivities were now complete and our game was soon underway. As far as I know, Feller never learned the real identity of the batter who defeated him that day. Hours later when our game was complete, Bob Feller was nowhere to be found. I bet he was back on the road to try his luck in the next baseball city.

"Hey, kid, just remember a few things. Be on time. Bust your butt. Play smart. And while you're at it have a few laughs."
— *Whitey Herzog, giving me his team rules prior to my major league debut*

Bottom of the Third

MAJOR LEAGUE DEBUT

I WALKED THROUGH THE clubhouse doors feeling like a kid entering Disney's Magic Kingdom for the first time—eyes huge and brimming with excitement, an ear-to-ear grin on my face, a spring in my step that had me nearly bouncing off the walls. I'd finally made it to "the show." My first day in the major leagues.

The date was August 5, 1986. The St. Louis Cardinals had just called me up from the Triple-A team in Louisville, Kentucky. The temperature on the Busch Stadium turf was a blazing 100 degrees, but that didn't matter. I was living my childhood dream and nothing could spoil it.

I dropped my bags at the cubicle located at the left of the doorway. Seeing my nametag, **MORRIS 33**, high atop the 3' x 6' locker, confirmed that I had indeed arrived. After a brief greeting from my new teammates I was given a quick tour of the facility by equipment manager Buddy Bates. I dressed quickly and shook hands with anyone that passed. I felt welcomed and appreciated.

I walked over to the wall near manager Whitey Herzog's office where the lineup was posted. Reading down the card, I couldn't believe my eyes. There was my name, batting sixth that evening, starting in right field. I had to give the card a second glance to make sure I wasn't dreaming. But it was true. I was just a few hours away from making my major league debut!

We were playing the Philadelphia Phillies that evening before an expected crowd of 40,000 fans. Butterflies fluttered in the bottom of my stomach. Like a teenager going on his first date, I was eager but anxious, intent on making an impression on the legions of Cardinal fans that would fill the stadium that night. If I had anything to say about it, everyone in the park would know who John Morris was before this game was over.

In the top of the first inning, pitcher Bob Forsch recorded three easy outs. I flew off the field, my legs barely touching the ground. Finding a spot in the dugout next to shortstop Ozzie Smith, I bubbled with excitement at finally making it to the major leagues. "Hey Oz, this is great. Is it this awesome all the time?"

Ozzie looked at me and nodded with approval as he carefully chose his words, "Relax, you've got a long game ahead of you and an even longer season. Just take it easy and enjoy the ride." Ozzie's comments went in one ear and right out the other. I felt too good to pull back the reins.

In the bottom of the first inning, we mounted a threat with basehits from Vince Coleman and Tommy Herr. However, they were stranded as the heart of the batting order failed to deliver. I was left on-deck when

Spring training in Clearwater, FL, after a two-hour rain delay, 1986.

Terry Pendleton's blast to the warning track was caught. No problem. I was determined to start another rally when it was my turn to lead off in the next inning.

I grabbed my glove and hustled out to right field to begin the second inning. The leadoff hitter was Mike Schmidt, one of the most prolific power hitters to ever play the game and certainly the most serious threat in the Phillies lineup that night. I knew he had the ability to drive the ball out of any part of the park.

I was ready—or so I thought. Forsch delivered the first pitch. A fastball over the outer half of the plate. Schmidt hacked at the offering. The ball shot straight up in the air. I *thought* the ball was hit in my direction—but I wasn't sure. The ball disappeared the second it left the bat. Gone. Nowhere to be seen. I knew it had to be somewhere above me as I looked towards the twilight sky, but I couldn't find it. Flailing my arms violently, I silently begged for help from anyone. But I stood alone waiting for the ball to reappear.

Suddenly, a loud thud from behind startled me. I snapped my head to the left and watched as the ball bounced high off the Astroturf some 30 feet behind me. The first ball ever hit towards me in the big leagues and I had completely butchered it. I chased after the ball as it rolled on the warning track, but Schmidt wound up on third base.

The fans were outraged. A chorus of thundering boos rang down on me, the likes of which I had never heard before. "Send him back to the minors" and "Hey Morris, if you had one more eye, you'd be a cy-

clops" were some of the *nicer* lines I heard over the next few minutes. I hadn't even batted yet and the normally reserved Cardinal faithful was running me out of town. But heck, if I were in the stands I would have done the same thing.

Suddenly, this cool, calm, cocky rookie had turned to jelly. There wasn't a hole small enough on the turf for me to crawl into. I was humiliated, embarrassed, and scared to death—a mere shell of the man who had walked so confidently into the clubhouse only hours earlier. A tightness gripped my body as the boos became louder. My knees shook uncontrollably, my feet felt glued to the turf, and my arms felt taped to the side of my body. My only wish was that the ball not come my way again—*ever.*

I managed to survive the rest of the inning without further incident. However, Schmidt did score the only run of the inning, thanks to my defensive blunder. And guess who got to make his major league batting debut, leading off the bottom half of the second?

The booing intensified again as I approached the batter's box. The fans didn't need the public address announcer to inform them who was leading off. Just sticking my head out of the dugout had been enough for them to let me have it one more time. The moment I had been waiting for all my life was upon me and it now felt like I was living my worst nightmare.

Impatiently, I swung at the first pitch, lofting a routine flyball to right field for out number one. After a momentary lull to follow the ball, the boos resumed, following me all the way back to the dugout. My head hung low. I wanted to run away, but there was nowhere to hide. There were still seven long innings to go. How was I going to survive? Judging by their reaction, I was convinced the fans never wanted to see me wear the Cardinals' uniform again.

I played like a statue for the remainder of the game—stiff, rigid, hoping the ball would be hit to someone else. During the fifth inning, Von Hayes—the best left-handed stick in the Phillies' lineup hit a routine flyball that I caught without incident. But the fans did not forgive or forget. Hundreds of fans along the right-field line gave me a mock standing ovation for the routine catch, unwilling to let go of my earlier miscue.

My next two plate appearances were anything but impressive as I did little to earn the fans favor. I looked like I belonged in the bush

Rookie year, August 1986.

leagues instead of the major leagues. We entered the bottom of the seventh inning, trailing by the same score of 1-0. We had to do something. If we lost, I would have to bare the responsibility for the only run of the game. You might as well ship me back to Triple-A to let me live out a miserable baseball career riding old buses, dressing in cramped clubhouses, and never advancing to the majors.

57

Fortunately, we rallied for five runs in the seventh inning and two in the eighth inning. Final score, 7-2. My major league debut was now complete but I would have been hard pressed to make a worse first impression on my manager, teammates, and the Cardinals' fans.

Ninety minutes later, I was across the street in the Marriott Hotel— my new home for the season. After entering my room on the 16th floor, I turned on the television, flipping the channel control to ESPN's *Sports Center.* Tom Mees, the program's anchor, was showing highlights of major league baseball games, beginning with the American League. After a couple of clips he made a smooth transition to the National League. "Let's take you to St. Louis, ladies and gentlemen," he began. "How about this for a major league debut?"

There it was again, haunting me like a bad dream. A full-color video replay of my spectacular error. The only thing missing was the thousands of boos from Cardinal fans. But Mees got on a roll, taking great pleasure in showing off the defensive miscue. "Watch right fielder John Morris as he plays this routine flyball into a three-base error." Alone in my bed, I could barely watch as Mees showed the replay a second time. But he wasn't finished just yet. Hoping to milk another laugh from viewers at my expense, Mees replayed the blooper for a third and final time. This time, it was too painful to watch. So I did what any normal embarrassed, humiliated, and humbled 25-year-old would do—I stuck my head under the covers so I wouldn't have to watch the pathetic display if Mees played it again.

Seconds later the phone rang. It was my older brother Andy calling from New York, and he had plenty to say. "Nice catch, Johnny. What the hell are you doing out there? I just saw you on ESPN. I think it's safe to say that the worst is over." Now there was no place left to hide. Everyone had seen it. Would I ever be able to live it down?

The next morning, I semi-skulked into the clubhouse for the afternoon contest. Secretly, I hoped I wouldn't be in the starting lineup so that the fans would have more time to forget about my less than stunning debut. However, manager Whitey Herzog had other ideas. Once

St. Louis Cardinals manager, Whitey Herzog. (Photo © St. Louis Baseball Cardinals)

again I was inserted into the starting lineup. I was being given a second chance—or was I being challenged? I only hoped Whitey knew what he was doing. Whatever the case, in my mind I was already hearing the boos.

The game began and in the first inning, I fielded two tough chances flawlessly, going deep into the gap to snag scorching line drives. Leading off the second inning, I heard only a smattering of boos scattered throughout the crowd. I worked the count to 2-0. Then righthander Kevin Gross delivered a thigh-high fastball that I stroked to right field for my first major league hit. I was relieved. The weight of the world had been lifted from my shoulders. I proceeded to steal second and third base on consecutive pitches before scoring on a sacrifice fly. Another hit and run came later in the game and we won the game by a score of 6-3. Final tally for the day; two hits, two stolen bases, and an RBI.

The boos from the previous night had been replaced by cheers and words of encouragement from both teammates and fans. As wonderful as the second game was, I soon realized that it was only one game, and that tomorrow would provide the opportunity to do it all over again. I guess Ozzie Smith was right when he offered those words of wisdom to me on the bench from the night before.

"It's a long season. Take it easy and enjoy the ride!"

East Side, West Side, ev'rybody's comin' down
To meet the M-E-T-S of New York town
                                    —*Ruth Roberts and Bill Katz*

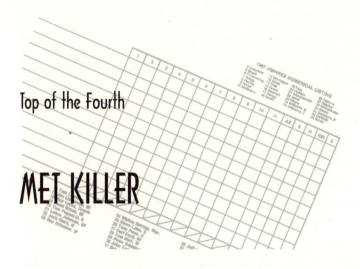

Top of the Fourth

MET KILLER

OUR EYES WERE GLUED to the black and white TV near the front of Ms. Molic's classroom. Most of us fidgeted nervously in our blue and orange T-shirts as Curt Gowdy's golden voice echoed through the Jacob Gunther Elementary School corridors. All of our teachers were treating us to Game Five of the 1969 World Series, featuring the New York Mets and the heavily favored Baltimore Orioles as Jerry Koosman, the Mets' veteran portsider, took a 4-1 lead into the ninth inning. With two outs, Orioles second baseman Davey Johnson lofted a flyball to Cleon Jones in left field as bedlam erupted at Shea Stadium. As Jones made the catch for the final out, pandemonium had already broken out inside our classroom. The "Miracle Mets" had become champions of the baseball world for the first time in their short history!

As we headed to junior high, and into the '70s when most of the Mets' teams were finishing between third and sixth place in the National League Eastern Division, I remained optimistic that another championship wasn't too far away. During those lean years I routinely made the 20-mile trek across Long Island to Flushing, Queens, to see

61

them play. My preference was to see the Mets play against Willie McCovey and the San Francisco Giants, while my brother Andy loved going to see Hank Aaron and the Atlanta Braves. Although my dad never admitted to having a favorite team, his eyes usually widened at the mere mention of Lou Brock and the St. Louis Cardinals. The three of us would pile into our family's green and brown paneled station wagon and make a day of it at the old ballyard. Dad usually bought us nose-bleed seats for two bucks apiece. We'd get there early enough for batting practice and watch the game from high above the action. Although the Mets didn't always prevail, the three of us always had a great time.

Years later in August 1986, my affection for the Mets took an abrupt turn when I showed up at Shea Stadium as a member of the St. Louis Cardinals—the Mets' most bitter rival. I had only been with the Cards for 10 days prior to the homecoming. Our team was floundering near the bottom of the Eastern Division, 18 games behind the front-running New Yorkers. The Mets were the "Beasts of the East" and they appeared ready to capture their first World Series flag since my days in the third grade. There was no doubt that "baseball magic" was back in the "Big Apple." The only difference was that heroes named Strawberry, Gooden, and Dykstra now replaced stars from years past— guys like Agee, Seaver, and Swoboda.

I had plenty of incentive to play well in my first visit at Shea. Pride and ego demanded that I impress family and friends, most of whom had not seen me hit a baseball since my college days at Seton Hall University. Also, in my short tenure with the team I had become aware of the nasty rivalry that festered between the two clubs. A war of words had begun in 1984 when the Mets reestablished themselves as serious pennant contenders. The tabloid rhetoric intensified in 1985 when the Cardinals captured the division crown, holding off the hard-charging Mets in the waning days of the season. Neither team held back when it came to attacking each another in print or on the air. Howard Johnson and Wally Backman taunted the Cardinals on a daily basis. Their verbal jabs consistently drew the ire of the Redbirds, especially players like

Danny Cox and Ozzie Smith. The rivalry had all the makings of a good soap opera—jealousy, trash talking, and intense competition.

On Thursday, August 14th I strolled onto the field, hours before batting practice. A sense of déjà vu overwhelmed me. I was standing comfortably on the very field that had provided so many wonderful childhood memories. But instead of a kid squinting through a pair of binoculars from the upper deck, I was now part of the action. The infield grass had the look of a well-manicured putting green. The grounds crew strategically placed cages and screens around the infield. Frank Sinatra's "New York, New York" boomed from gigantic speakers inside the 80-foot scoreboard in right field. The IRT Local roared in the distance just behind the stadium parking lot and 727's from nearby LaGuardia Airport thundered above the stadium every few minutes. Television crews stayed busy laying yards of cable around both dugouts. And Gary Carter, the Mets' All-Star catcher, put the final touches on a television commercial while several of his teammates entertained local scribes in the dugout. It was a New York kind of day all the way. Plenty of noise, and the first pitch had yet to be thrown.

I started game one of the twi-night doubleheader in right field against Ron Darling. The Ivy Leaguer relied on pinpoint control and a variety of off-speed pitches to keep hitters off balance. Many hitters regarded his forkball as the best in the league. I took the collar in the game, going 0-4 with two weak grounders, a lazy flyball, and a strikeout. I took solace in that there were still five games left to play in the series. I grabbed a seat on the bench for the nightcap. But one thing I learned quickly about playing for Whitey Herzog was that you never knew when he'd insert one of his bench players into the game.

We trailed by two runs entering the seventh inning as 50,000 hometown fanatics screamed at the thought of a doubleheader sweep. Suddenly, the command came from Whitey. "Johnny, go to right field." I grabbed my glove and sprinted out of the dugout. Several minutes later, in the bottom of the frame I lined a single to left and scored three batters later on Willie McGee's basehit. In the ninth, lefty-closer Jesse

63

Orosco entered the game to preserve the Mets' lead. After a quick out, Orosco loaded the bases with a pair of singles and a walk. I was the next scheduled batter, but I realized that this was a classic textbook opportunity for Whitey to make a pinch-hitting move. The "White Rat," a name the skipper received in his playing days for his light hair and street savvy smarts, was regarded as one of the premiere strategists in the game. He was a master at utilizing his bench when the game was on the line. So I was somewhat surprised when he left me in to hit against Orosco. I wondered if maybe I was being tested. Maybe Whitey just wanted to see how I would handle a dose of big league pressure in front of the hometown folks.

A hit would give us the lead. I suspected Orosco would try to get ahead with a fastball. I guessed right. His belt-high offering over the inner third of the plate was just the pitch I was looking for. The ball jumped off my bat, took one hard bounce off the infield dirt, and skipped between second baseman Tim Teufel and first baseman Keith Hernandez into right field. One run scored to tie the game and Terry Pendleton followed from second base with the go-ahead run. Darryl Strawberry uncorked a wild throw in the direction of homeplate that missed so badly it sent season ticketholders diving for cover in the stands. The misguided missile plated a third run and allowed me to wind up at third base.

The lead may have been ours but the game was far from over. In the bottom of the ninth the Mets rallied by loading the bases against our closer Todd Worrell. Chants of "Let's go Mets" filled the stadium as Gary Carter strutted to the plate. Carter had made a career out of coming through in these pressure situations, but despite that reputation, Worrell challenged and blew him away with a series of high fastballs to preserve the win.

Whitey penciled my name back in the lineup the following day. Hours before we needed to be on the field for batting practice I stood over a table in the clubhouse and scribbled my signature on six dozen baseballs. Then I made sure that all 35 names on my pass list were entered on the appropriate sign-in sheet. Sports sections from several newspapers littered the table. At the top of one pile was the back page of the *New York Daily News.* The tabloid had for decades been a favorite for New York sports fans. I fondly remembered as a teenager digesting as much sports information as I could when I delivered the newspaper to neighborhood subscribers on my pre-dawn route.

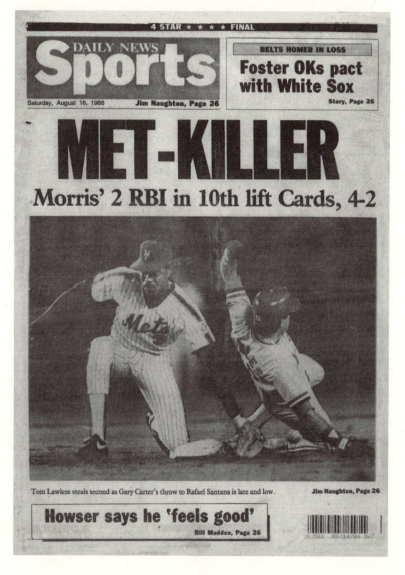

4 STAR ★ ★ ★ FINAL

DAILY NEWS
Sports

BELTS HOMER IN LOSS
Foster OKs pact with White Sox
Story, Page 26

Saturday, August 16, 1986   Jim Naughton, Page 26

MET-KILLER
Morris' 2 RBI in 10th lift Cards, 4-2

Tom Lawless steals second as Gary Carter's throw to Rafael Santana is late and low.   Jim Naughton, Page 26

Howser says he 'feels good'
Bill Madden, Page 26

In big block letters, the headline caught my eye. **"MET KILLER"** covered the top half of the page while a picture of Tom Lawless sliding safely into second base took up the bottom half. I scratched my head for several seconds before I realized the headline was referring to me. At first I couldn't figure out if I was being painted as one of the city's most wanted criminals or just as a royal pain in the ass for New York's favorite team. But as I thumbed my way through the pages I realized it was the latter. One article gave a glowing account of my game-winning hit the night before while another article chronicled my life as an athlete growing up in the shadows of Shea Stadium. The stories did a nice job of stroking my ego, but I knew there was still plenty of baseball to be played in this series. By the time the game ended later that evening, I had three more hits and helped our team snatch another win.

Whitey threw me back into the starting lineup on Saturday afternoon. After nine innings of trading runs the score was tied as we headed into extra innings. In the top of the 10th, I came to the plate with a runner on third and two outs. Roger McDowell, the Mets' sinkerball specialist, was on the hill. After the count reached two balls and two strikes McDowell hung me a slider. I jumped all over the mistake offering and drilled it inside the first-base bag past Lee Mazzilli for a go-ahead triple. Minutes later, Worrell came on to record his second save in as many days. After the game ended I was whisked away to a small room buried beneath the stadium stands to be a guest on "Kiner's Corner." This was the same Mets' post-game show that had been on WOR-TV since I was barely able to stand and whack crab apples with a whiffle ball bat in my backyard. Half an hour later I sat beside a mountain of television cameras and microphones, fielding questions from the inquiring minds of New York's top sportswriters. I basked in the "Big Apple" limelight and loved every minute of it. Later that evening there were dozens of phone calls and house visits from friends and neighbors. People I hadn't heard from in years, maybe since Ms. Molic's class, wanted to talk about old times. I wondered if 35 passes would be enough for the next game.

The last day of the series was a Sunday doubleheader. Dwight Gooden, the Mets' ace hurler, was on the mound in the opener. In Gooden's first few years in the majors, his overpowering fastball and pinpoint control established him as the premiere pitcher in the league. So when I saw my name in the starting lineup I knew that my greatest big league challenge was upon me. Fortunately, we jumped on Gooden early and by the fourth inning he was headed for the showers. By the time our victory was sealed I had banged out two more hits, giving me eight for the series. Sid Fernandez, the Mets' hefty lefthander, shut us down in the nightcap with a stellar pitching performance. I fidgeted on the bench the entire game hoping for one last shot at victory. But you don't always get what you wish for.

Ninety minutes after the final out, our charter plane left LaGuardia Airport for St. Louis. As I reclined in my seat with an Anheuser Busch product in my hand, I beamed with confidence knowing I had played a major role in our success against the Mets. A highlight reel flicked on in my head and I began to replay my game-winning hits over the past few days. While my body melted into the seat I began, for no apparent reason, to daydream about some of the spectacular moments of the 1969 Miracle Mets. I envisioned Tom Seaver and his dominating pitching performances, which included a club record 25 wins and his first Cy Young Award. I saw the Mets storm back from a nine-and-a-half game deficit in mid-August to catch the Cubs for the Eastern Division crown. And, of course, I rehashed all the countless times I sat with my brother and dad, listening to Ralph Kiner, Lindsey Nelson, and Bob Murphy describe the action to the tri-state area.

Two months after my first series at Shea, the Mets would have the last laugh, winning the World Series against the Boston Red Sox in a thrilling seven-game series. I had tickets for Game Six, and I sat 50 rows behind the Mets' dugout on a chilly October night. It turned out to be a game that will be remembered as one of the greatest comebacks in World Series history. Champagne was already on ice in the Red Sox' clubhouse. One more out and the Red Sox would have their first World Series championship since Babe Ruth left the team in 1918. But with two outs and nobody on base, the Mets staged a gut-wrenching rally and won the game. Although many baseball fans have tried to pin the Red Sox' demise on Bill Buckner's game-ending error, I suspected that the heart of the Mets' team and some baseball magic had been the main ingredients in bringing the Mets their second World Series championship the following night.

As an eight-year-old, and now as a 25-year-old, I had witnessed both of the miracle seasons for the Mets. But sandwiched between them was my own dream come true. It was a chance for me to come home and take center stage against the best team in the land—"The Amazing Mets."

(Photo courtesy of the National Baseball Hall of Fame Library, Cooperstown, NY)

"The Cardinals of the 1980s had hitting, pitching, speed and determination. But that was not why we won. We won because of Whitey Herzog. He just seemed to know what was going to happen next, who would do what. He had an instinct, an intuition I'd never seen before."

—*Ozzie Smith*

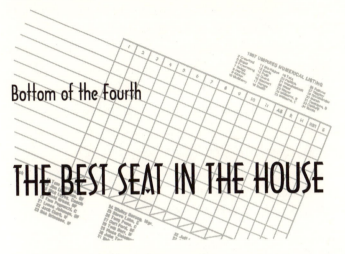

Bottom of the Fourth

THE BEST SEAT IN THE HOUSE

THE DOCTORS SAID THEY found a grapefruit-size tumor in his lungs. I guess I shouldn't have been surprised. My dad, John Mathew Morris, had been a two-pack-a-day guy for the better part of 40 years. He loved his "cancer sticks," and maybe now he was paying the ultimate price for all those years of abuse.

It was April of the 1987 baseball season when I received the news about Dad. When I'd left home months earlier, Dad's spirits were high, his sense of humor intact, and his health appeared to be fine. But life has a way of changing quickly.

Mom called to tell me the bad news. As soon as I heard, a cold wave passed through my body and my mind went numb with sadness. Instantly, I wanted to be transported home, to see him, to comfort him. But I was a thousand miles from home and I knew there was little I could do for him. So I continued doing what I could do: I played baseball to the best of my ability so Dad could feel proud of his son.

Meanwhile, our team, the St. Louis Cardinals, was serving notice to the rest of the National League that we were a force to be reckoned with—a team that had a good chance of winning the pennant and World Series. That's how good our team was, and we knew it.

The doctors made it clear that due to the advanced state of the cancer, there was little hope of Dad's survival, but they would do their best. The prognosis was not good and everyone knew it, including Dad. He went through the standard battery of tests and treatments for cancer—X- rays, blood work, and radiation treatment. From the description my family gave me, it sounded like he was being used as an experimental guinea pig. He turned into a human pincushion. Black and blue marks covered his arms from the many IV tubes that were stuck in his veins. But in the end, we were told that Dad had only several months to live. At the urging of the doctors, he was admitted to a hospice facility so he would be as comfortable as possible in his final days.

As the baseball season progressed, the Cardinals built a commanding 10-game lead heading into the All-Star break. We were operating on all cylinders—like a well-oiled machine. We received stellar pitching from our starters; Tudor, Cox, Forsch, Magrane, and Mathews kept us in the majority of our games. We played sharp defense on a daily basis, and our lineup produced an exciting brand of offense. Featuring tremendous speed from top to bottom, the "Running Redbirds" were masters of putting pressure on the defense. Taking the extra base on routine hits, stealing bases, and executing the "hit and run" were strategies we used in beating other teams into submission. Coleman, Smith, McGee, Pendleton, and Herr were all prolific basestealers. Their thievery became the talk of the National League.

The one thing our lineup lacked as a whole was power. Mostly, we were a group of line-drive hitters with the speed of a gazelle and the guts of a burglar.

But we did have one player in our lineup who packed some serious thunder in his bat—Jack Clark. He stood an imposing 6'4" and weighed 230 pounds. His dark features and stern looks could unnerve many an opposing pitcher. He was tough. He was straightforward. And we all loved him. "Jack the Ripper" was taking the league by storm that

Jack Clark. (Photo © St. Louis Baseball Cardinals, Steven Goldstein photo)

season. His awesome home-run power struck fear in the opposition. Anytime we needed a big hit, it seemed that Clark would produce either a scorching line drive or one of his monstrous home runs.

Yes, baseball was fun that summer. Fast, exciting, and exhilarating. Just the way it was supposed to be. Our team, with its power hitter surrounded by eight jackrabbits with blazing speed, had a winning combination and a mission to get the pennant.

We came to New York to play the Mets immediately following the All-Star break. It had been four months since my last visit, so before each game of the weekend series I drove the length of the Long Island Expressway to visit Dad at the Suffolk County hospice facility.

While we were together, our conversations centered on baseball and the Cardinals. Dad loved baseball. It was his one true passion in life. As a matter of fact, he had been quite a player himself back in the 1920s when he played first base for a semi-pro team. He was a slick-

John Morris standing far left, 1929.

fielding, sure-handed defensive player who handled himself well with the bat.

The three-game series gave us some quality time together. Dad's face would light up at the mention of the Cardinals and how we were dominating the competition. I felt good knowing I was bringing some joy into a life that was now full of pain and struggle.

He was a proud father who, given the fact that his youngest son was playing major league baseball, liked to show me off to all the nurses and doctors when I visited. He loved telling them that his son was a major leaguer. As embarrassed as it made me, I just played along, letting him enjoy the attention.

But the visits were difficult and sad. I was emotionally drained each day after leaving him. It was hard to watch this proud man shrivel up into nothing. The cancer had really taken hold of him and each time I wondered if it would be the last time I'd see him alive.

For each game, Dad managed to muster up enough energy to watch our series on TV. The series developed into a heated three-game set between two longtime rivals. The Cardinals were National League champs two years earlier, while the Mets were the defending World Series champs.

These were two teams that were used to winning plus they hated one another. As usual, a war of words had been building in the media, and this series was providing enough quotes and insults in the New York tabloids to incite a riot.

The series was a nail-biter as the Mets took two of the three games from us. Our once insurmountable lead had shrunk to six games with barely two months remaining in the season. The Mets and the rest of the division were ready to make their move. Just the kind of thing my Dad loved watching: competitive baseball, two gladiators going at it.

Two months later, in the middle of September, we returned to Shea Stadium to play a pivotal series against the Mets. The series would play a huge role in determining the Eastern Division championship. Our lead had been reduced to one game, and the Mets were showing the

73

entire country why they were the defending World Champions. These guys would not go down easy. They would be in it until the end, and we knew it.

During the series, I stayed with Mom and my brother Andy. There was a great deal going on in my head—Dad's failing health, the pressure of a pennant race, and our lead slipping away. But I felt great physically. The excitement of being in a pennant race in my first full major league season kept me energized. For the first time, I was using baseball to bring some sense of joy to a sad situation. I played each day with the hope that it would allow Dad to think of something else other than his illness. As it turned out, it helped Dad, the rest of the family, and me.

I was able to visit with Dad all three days, just as I had done on the previous trip in July, but these visits were much different. It was not a pretty sight. Dad was in a helpless state, both physically and mentally. He weighed about 100 pounds and was unable to walk or talk. His body was all skin and bones. But each day a nurse would wheel Dad into a large room, his red Cardinals' hat proudly displayed atop his sunken head. I talked about the team, and how we were trying to hold off the hard-charging Mets. But all he could do was nod his head in agreement.

It was difficult to stay long. Seeing him in that condition was overwhelming. It was almost too much for me to handle. Everyday before I left his hospital room to go to the stadium, there was one thing Dad would communicate to me: scribbling on a note pad, he'd write that he'd be watching our game that night on TV.

Friday night. Game one of the series. We trailed the Mets by one run in the ninth inning. Two outs with a runner at first. Terry Pendleton, our third baseman, at the plate facing Roger McDowell, the closer for the Mets. One more out and the Mets would tie us for the division lead. Fifty thousand fans are going crazy over the prospect of the Mets catching us. Like crazed animals they were on their feet, chanting and screaming as McDowell was ready to put the finishing touches on another Mets' victory.

But McDowell made a mistake—one that resulted in one of the greatest hits in Cardinals' history. A sinker that didn't sink low enough. Pendleton connected with the knee-high pitch, sending a thunderous bomb to dead-center field. Mookie Wilson retreated to the base of the wall only to see the ball disappear into the night for a game-winning home run.

The next day we pounced on Dwight Gooden for five runs in the first before cruising to an easy win. Whatever momentum the Mets had built before we came to town had vanished. The following afternoon we played in the rain, a six-hour contest interrupted several times by heavy storms. We lost, but the damage inflicted upon the Mets was already complete.

Meanwhile, back on Long Island, Dad was watching. Whatever energy he had left in his shrunken body was spent watching the contest. But they were to be his last games. Three days after the final out at Shea, we arrived in Pittsburgh to play the Pirates. A knock at my hotel door in the early morning hours startled me. "Johnny, it's Whitey." Right then I thought to myself, "Dad's gone."

I flew home that Wednesday afternoon for the wake and burial of my dad. I'd known this day was coming for some time, but that knowledge in no way eased the hurt. He was laid to rest on Saturday afternoon. Afterwards, I met with my family and I asked them if they wanted me to stay longer. Unanimously, they urged me to go back and help the Cardinals finish the remaining two weeks of the season.

I made travel arrangements for a return to St. Louis the following morning. Our team was clinging to a precious one-game lead over the Mets. Twelve games remained in the season and I hoped my return would help the team in the stretch drive.

Sunday morning began with a 4:30 wake-up call. Plenty of time to drive to LaGuardia Airport for the 6:30 to St. Louis. But there was only one problem—the flight was cancelled and I was left unsure if I could make it to Busch Stadium for the start of the afternoon game against the Chicago Cubs. But somebody was on my side that day. A seat opened up on a flight later that morning, allowing me to arrive in St. Louis at 11:30. Next stop, Busch Stadium.

Entering the clubhouse I was greeted warmly by teammates and coaches. As I began to dress, Dave Ricketts, our bullpen coach, walked over to my locker. "Johnny, Whitey wants to see you." I walked to the skipper's office not knowing what to expect. I noticed that the lineup card was missing from its usual spot on the wall adjacent to Whitey's office. That seemed odd.

After I turned the corner into his office, Whitey rose from behind his desk to greet me, "Hey kid, it's nice to have ya back. Look, I know there's nothing more trying than a funeral and that you've been through hell the past few days." He paused slightly before retrieving something from the top of his desk. He turned back to me, his face reflecting both support and concern. He extended both of his hands, a lineup card in each. "Johnny, I'm gonna leave it up to you. I've made out two lineups cards. One has you starting and the other has you on the bench in case you're not ready yet. Whatever you decide is fine with me."

I couldn't believe what I was hearing. A string of questions exploded in my head. Was Whitey actually waiting for me before he was going to post the lineup? Was I dreaming? Was he really serious with this unusual offer? Slowly, it dawned on me that Whitey was offering me a challenge. At the same time he also was showing compassion for me as a human being.

Finally I responded: "Whitey, I just flew 1,000 miles this morning to get here. I'd love to play today." Whitey smiled with approval and extended his hand. "Great, you're in there. Now go out and get a few hits for your dad."

It was 12:30, game time less than 45 minutes away. I'd just had four days of inactivity—no batting practice, no throwing, or running—and I was being thrown right back into the fire, into the thick of the pennant race. So much for sitting around and feeling sorry for myself.

I stepped onto the field several minutes prior to the first pitch. A quiet peace had settled over me, creating energy from head to toe. I knew what Whitey was doing. He was providing me with a wonderful opportunity. Being in the starting lineup that day was truly a gift.

I played right field on that beautiful Sunday afternoon and batted seventh in the lineup. In the bottom of the first inning I got my first chance as I came to the plate with the bases loaded. Righthander Greg Maddux was the pitcher. He was an up-and-coming star who'd mastered a variety of pitches. With the count two balls and two strikes, Maddux hung a slider and I drove in the first two runs of the game with a single to center field.

In the third inning, I batted with a runner on third base. A routine groundball out to the shortstop drove in the run, allowing us to increase the lead to 3-0. I came to the plate again in the bottom half of the eighth inning. With two outs and a man on second base, I had another chance to drive in a run. After falling behind in the count, reliever Mike Mason threw a fastball over the heart of the plate. My head stayed still as I tracked it all the way. A short smooth stroke, usually the type reserved for the Tony Gywnn's and the Paul Molitor's of the world, sent another line drive single to center field. My fourth RBI of the day! Our lead was now at 7-2.

Though I could have no idea that these four RBI were a career high, I did know that I had just done something special. The fans knew about my loss and the crowd of 46,681 stood in unison to acknowledge my performance and to lend their love and support in my time of grief. While I stood on first base and listened to their applause, the ovation seemed to last forever. A lump formed in my throat as a mixture of joy and sorrow swelled inside me. I realized I had just paid Dad the greatest tribute I could have given him. With both feet firmly planted on top of first base, my eyes glistened as tears ran freely down my cheeks. I glanced upward and seeing the gorgeous blue skies, I suddenly had an image of Dad smiling down on me with approval and pride, content in the fact that his youngest son was winning the game he loved. Dad was indeed watching over me that day, and his vantage point provided him with the best seat in the house.

Days later, we clinched the division title from the Mets and a week later we knocked off the San Francisco Giants in a thrilling seven-game series to become National League champions. It was now off to the World Series to play the Minnesota Twins. It was an evenly played Series that would come down to the seventh and deciding game. We gave it our best shot, but came up short, losing Game Seven by a score of 4-2. The season was now complete, and so was my relationship with Dad—all because Whitey Herzog gave me the chance to say a special farewell to my biggest fan.

"Sounds to me like he's trying to drum up some business for his new restaurant."

—Joe Magrane, responding to complaints from Whitey Herzog that his players don't have enough grease and fat in their diets

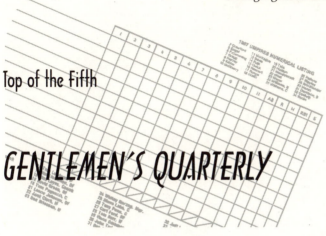

Top of the Fifth

GENTLEMEN'S QUARTERLY

GROWING UP, HIS FAVORITE baseball player was Hall-of-Fame pitcher Steve Carlton. He carefully studied and emulated Carlton's pitching motion and, like Carlton, brought an intense spirit of competition to the mound when it was his turn to pitch. His most effective pitch was his sinking fastball. When it was working well, he could throw it at the middle of the plate and use the ball's movement to disrupt a batter's timing. Hitters complained that his ball sunk so much, it felt as if they were hitting a brick whenever they did make contact. He also fielded his position flawlessly and took great pride in developing his bunting and hitting skills. His name was Joe Magrane. I got to play baseball with him for the St. Louis Cardinals between 1986 and 1990.

A tall striking man with the looks of a male model, Joe stood 6'5," weighed approximately 250 pounds, and was in excellent shape. He had huge hands and a handshake that warned of enormous physical strength. Thick blond hair that flowed easily to the side and ocean blue eyes complemented his oval face. Cardinals fans admired not only his

Joe Magrane relaxing at Al Lang Stadium, spring training, 1989. (Photo credit: PF Sports Images)

good looks but also his winning record. The press flocked to him because they could count on him to provide a quick, humorous quote.

Three days a week, he clowned with the disk jockeys on a local rock station and fielded phone calls from music and baseball fans. Joe often stated that when he retired from baseball, he wanted to become a radio or TV broadcaster. During games, he would sit in the dugout and work on his play-by-play and his radio/TV voice. He often imitated some of the top game announcers, including Vince Scully, Jack Buck, and Harry Kalas. Joe was able to mimic their powerful voices to perfection.

Off the field, Joe had a very sharp sense of humor—which he didn't hesitate to put to use at the expense of his teammates. He was an expert at pulling practical jokes and, more importantly, getting away with them. A favorite trick of his was the toilet paper bomb. On road trips to Southern California, players would often lounge next to the hotel pool and soak up the sun. Joe would take the opportunity to soak a large wad of toilet paper, then launch it out a 15th-story hotel window towards an unsuspecting teammate. Once, in the minor leagues, Joe managed to steal a teammate's hotel key. When the teammate retired for the night, he found his bed sheets gone, all the light bulbs missing, and the mouthpiece removed from the phone so he couldn't call the front desk. To top it off, when the player tried to leave the room, he discovered his door jammed from the outside. From Ben Gay spread in players' jock straps to smoke bombs in lockers, Joe did it all.

So it wasn't surprising that after years of abuse, several of Joe's teammates decided that they had had enough of his warped sense of humor and plotted their revenge. I am happy to say that I not only witnessed and enjoyed what many still consider the most original and well-planned practical joke in the history of major league baseball, but I also took part in its execution.

In 1988, our Cardinal team was going through a miserable season. By the beginning of August, thanks to injuries and poor performance, we were mired in last place. Joe continued to pitch aggressively and with enthusiasm, but was left with a losing record due to a lack of support from our anemic offense.

Near the end of August, Tom Brunansky, an outfielder, and Ozzie Smith, our shortstop, held a summit to come up with a prank to play on Joe. They decided that the best way to set Joe up would be to feed his ego.

Joe had a great interest in men's fashions and took pride in his physical appearance. As he dressed and groomed himself after the games, he was often seen admiring himself in clubhouse mirrors. An avid reader of several men's fashion magazines, he was frequently spotted around town sporting the latest styles. His favorite magazine was *Gentlemen's Quarterly*. Joe usually had several back issues of the magazine stuffed in his locker.

Brunansky set the plan in motion by placing a phone call to Joe at the stadium. Disguising his voice, Brunansky pretended to be an executive from *GQ* magazine and he asked Joe if he would be interested in being part of a photo shoot to take place at St. Louis' Busch Stadium the following day. The shoot would be a photo spread in the upcoming autumn edition. Joe bit. Excited by the prospect, he couldn't wait to get to the stadium the next day for his chance to make fashion history.

The following afternoon, many members of the team had already gathered in the clubhouse when Joe arrived. Carrying a garment bag containing an assortment of fall suits and heavy wool sweaters, Joe looked poised and confident. He began by dressing in a sharp-looking black suit. After carefully grooming himself and admiring his image in the full-length mirror next to his locker, he walked out the clubhouse door and onto the field. The temperature that day had already topped 90 degrees, but bright sunshine, high humidity, and Astroturf combined to make the playing field feel more like 110 degrees. As Joe strode out to right field, his teammates wondered how he would hold up in the afternoon heat.

The photographers—hired by Ozzie Smith—began the session by having Joe pose in the sweltering heat for 45 minutes. Dripping with

Ozzie Smith. (Photo credit: PF Sports Images)

Top of the Fifth

perspiration, Joe returned to the clubhouse and began changing into his favorite green pinstriped threads. It was my job to prod him a little, to get a sense of his feelings. I approached him, doing my best to bite back a smile.

"Joe," I asked, "how's it going out there?"

"Pretty good so far," he replied, quietly. "They want me to try on a few more outfits, so I may be out there a few more hours."

I was having a hard time believing that Joe was actually falling for this charade, but I continued to play along.

"So," I said, "I take it that *GQ* is paying a lot for your work. Come on, Joe, you can tell me, how much are they paying you?"

I sensed that Joe wished I would vanish. Nervously, he replied, "My agent hasn't worked out the specifics but it should be good. I gotta go, they're waiting for me on the field."

A few minutes after resuming the shoot, the entire team huddled near the corner of the dugout for a peek at Joe's exhibition. For the next two hours, Joe sprinted in and out of the clubhouse changing into every garment he'd brought with him. The session finally ended around 4 in the afternoon as the team readied itself for batting practice. As the photographers left the field, I saw one of them wink at Ozzie suggesting that everything had gone according to plan.

As humorous as the events were on that hot August afternoon, the real fun began some days later.

We played three more home games before beginning a week-long road trip. In Houston, we split the first two games against the Astros. Just prior to the start of the third game, Whitey Herzog called a team meeting in the clubhouse. Just as the meeting was about to begin, a clubhouse attendant burst through the clubhouse doors. "I've got a message for Joe Magrane," he said.

Taking the letter with a suspicious look, Joe opened it and began reading it to himself. It was clear by the expression on his face that the news was not good. Written on official *GQ* stationery, the letter said:

Dear Joe:

Due to your sub-par season, your pictorial spread for *GQ* magazine will not be used in the near future. We appreciate your efforts and we wish you the best of luck in your career.

As Joe read the letter, Ozzie Smith and Tom Brunansky hid in the corner of the clubhouse giggling like two little school children. They seemed to be taking particular pleasure in watching Joe suffer.

Several days later, we were in Atlanta to play the Braves. Whitey called another team meeting. Several minutes into the meeting, a young clubhouse attendant entered with a letter in his hand. "Message for Joe Magrane," he said.

Joe was seated on a nearby bench. As Joe took the letter, the attendant added, "The sender requested that you read it out loud."

Again, it was a note typed on official *GQ* stationery. As Joe examined the letter, his face turned a brilliant crimson. His body stiffened and he lowered his chin to his chest, muttering the words to himself. Finally, with a sigh, Joe slowly rose to his feet. He managed a weak smile, but embarrassment was clearly written on his face. Taking his time, Joe cleared his throat and began to read in a loud, clear voice.

Dear Joe:
Roses are red.
Violets are blue.
You've been had by your teammates.
There is no *GQ!*

The clubhouse exploded with the sound of uncontrolled laughter. Joe tried his best to hide his humiliation, but he knew he'd been had. The finishing touches had been applied to a masterful prank and everyone had a good laugh at Joe Magrane's expense.

Within a week, word of the practical joke played on Joe Magrane had leaked to many national news publications. Several, including

USA Today and The Sporting News, gave extensive coverage to the story. The media tried, but failed to discover the pranksters who had masterminded the event. It was a great joke, perfectly executed, but we could not have dreamed of the way the events would eventually play themselves out.

The following March, our team was training in St. Petersburg, Florida, preparing for the 1989 season. Joe was pitching well, determined to improve on his 1988 record. The GQ prank was by now a distant memory, but Joe still occasionally smarted from occasional good-natured kidding from both teammates and fans.

On the morning of March 20th with the entire team preoccupied with practice on the field, Joe launched an unforeseen counteroffensive. Secretly, he worked his way back to the clubhouse. Personally opening every copy to page 82, he distributed the April edition of GQ magazine at every player's locker.

As players returned to the clubhouse for the lunch break, they discovered Joe's gift. Page 82 was the beginning of a photo spread featuring Joe as the model. Many players sat in stunned silence as they reviewed eight pages featuring Joe Magrane modeling the men's spring fashion collection.

It turned out that after news stories about the original joke became public, representatives from the real GQ magazine contacted Joe and expressed genuine interest in doing a real photo spread. Over the course of the winter months, Joe had secretly worked out his retaliatory strike with its editors.

As I prepared for the afternoon's game at Al Lang Stadium, I glanced over at Joe. He sat in the corner of the locker room, a 500-watt smile plastered all over his face. Nodding in my direction, the Cardinals' ruling prankster, Joe Magrane. beamed and showed us all that the last laugh is the sweetest.

"Has the best arm I've ever seen in my life. Could be a real power pitcher some day."

—Red Murff, from a scouting report on a high school pitcher named Nolan Ryan

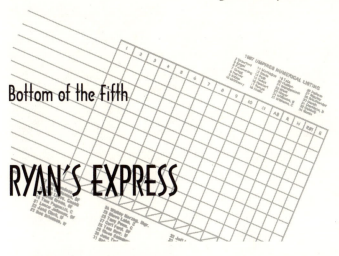

Bottom of the Fifth

RYAN'S EXPRESS

DURING NOLAN RYAN'S 27-year major league career he won 324 games and became the all-time leader in strikeouts with 5,714. The Hall-of-Famer from the Lone Star State is universally regarded as one of the most domineering and competitive human beings ever to set foot on a pitcher's mound.

After spending his first dozen years in the majors with the New York Mets and the California Angels, Ryan inked a three-year contract with the Houston Astros, and became baseball's first-million-dollar-a-year player in 1980. During the 1983 season he broke Walter Johnson's all-time strikeout record. If anyone had visions of Ryan slowing down as he approached age 40, they were grossly mistaken. Ryan had plenty of firepower left and he continued to terrorize batters until the day he retired.

The Ryan work ethic was for decades the envy of both teammates and adversaries alike. After every game pitched he would hold court with the media in the middle of the clubhouse while riding a stationary bike. For close to an hour Ryan would peddle away while fielding

Nolan Ryan. (Photo credit: PF Sports Images)

questions about his performance and his career. Such was the case even after tossing the record-breaking seventh no-hitter of his career. While most pitchers might have been slugging down beers or spraying champagne, Ryan patiently answered questions with poise and grace, while still getting his work done.

Ryan complemented his great work ethic with an unshakable belief in himself and the steely-eyed nerve of a western gunslinger. One steamy summer night, in the final year of his career, Ryan etched in the minds of baseball fans a lasting image of his toughness while pitching against the Chicago White Sox. Early in the game Robin Ventura, one of the Sox' best hitters, stepped into the batter's box. Ryan threw inside, actually way inside, nailing him in the ribs with a heater clocked in the mid-90s. Though unhurt physically, emotionally Ventura was beside himself. Every notion of common sense deserted his body as he threw down his bat and charged the mound. One would suspect that a 20-year-age gap would give Ventura the upper hand in a fight. But Nolan Ryan was not your typical 44-year-old. Ventura cocked his fist and threw a vicious right hook at Ryan's head and caught nothing but air. Ryan stood his ground as Ventura stumbled and lost his balance. Within seconds Ryan had Ventura in a headlock and was feeding the White Sox slugger the proverbial knuckle sandwich. After a group consultation, the umpires decided to keep Ryan in the game but eject Ventura for initiating the brawl. Ryan had scored a knockout for baby boomers and middle-aged men across the land. The favorite son of the Great State of Texas had indeed dropped a bomb on the Generation Xers of the world.

"Ferocious competitor" doesn't quite do justice to what I saw in Ryan one day in St. Louis. Cardinals stolen base king Vince Coleman started the game with a basehit to center field. Ryan attempted to pick him off no less than a dozen times in succession. It was obvious that Ryan was trying to wear the master thief out. Nevertheless, Coleman stole second base on Ryan's first pitch to the plate. Ryan pounded his fist into his glove, then took it upon himself to make sure Coleman wouldn't try to steal third base too. As Coleman took his lead Ryan suddenly spun off the rubber and fired a laser towards second base. This time, as Coleman slid into the bag, the ball smoked him squarely in his back, leaving him writhing on the ground. Coleman lay in pain near the base for several minutes. Finally rising and dusting himself off, it was clear Coleman was smarting from Ryan's target practice, and that he would not be stealing again in the near future. I was not quite clear whether or not Ryan was deliberately trying to drill Coleman. But in hindsight, it is crystal clear that Ryan would find a way to shut down any opponent.

Until the tail end of the 1988 season I had not yet had the chance to bat against the legendary superstar. It seemed every time the Cardinals faced Ryan's Astros during my first three major league seasons, he had either just pitched in the previous series or was injured.

That September, I entered the Astrodome clubhouse and checked the lineup like I did every day. I was excited about a possible start, but once again I would be riding the pine for at least the first six innings. After I mumbled a few choice words under my breath, Jim Lindeman, my closest friend on the team, patted me on the back and offered a few words of encouragement: "Relax. Whitey hasn't forgotten about you. You'll be in there before you know it."

Grabbing a bag of sunflower seeds, I took my usual seat near the far end of the dugout. I watched Ryan carefully while he took his first inning warm-up pitches. He didn't appear to be throwing very hard. However, once the game started I watched him blow away Vince Coleman, Willie McGee, and Tommy Herr with heaters clocked between 94 and 98 miles per hour! Batting left-handed, McGee's tardy swing on the first pitch laced a screaming missile into our third-base dugout—sending players and coaches running for cover. It was the only contact the threesome made the entire inning.

After Herr swung through another fastball to end the inning, I glared at Lindeman with mock disgust. "Are we trying?" I sneered. Lindeman's stern look issued a warning as he pointed a finger in my face. "Hey, wake up—we're facing Nolan Ryan, not Meg Ryan."

In the bottom of the first, our starting pitcher, Greg Matthews, immediately ran into trouble, loading the bases with a pair of hits and a walk. Glenn Davis, the Astros' most dangerous hitter, promptly emptied the bases with a double to the left-center field gap. Three more extra basehits followed. The rout was on. The Astros sent 13 men to the plate that inning and plated 10 runs to blow the game wide open.

As the Astros conducted their first inning track meet around the bases, I had plenty of time to get comfortable. But that would change quickly. Before the second out was recorded I noticed Whitey ambling towards me from the other end of the dugout. Then he was standing over me with a smile creasing his face. " Hey kid, we're getting our stinkin' butts kicked. I'm gonna get the starters outta there. I want you to lead off next inning, then stay in the game and go to right field." Whitey continued barking out instructions over the next 60 seconds. By the time the second inning began, Whitey's "bird turds"—a name the extra players had given themselves—had invaded the game.

Semi-stunned, I jumped off the bench and sent sunflower seeds flying in all directions. I accidentally smashed my head against the overhead equipment shelf. As I struggled to find my glove, bat, and helmet I was now in a mild state of panic. Finally, feeling a bump forming on the top of my head, I jogged down the long, narrow runway to take a few practice swings off a batting tee, knowing that in a few minutes I would get my chance against Nolan Ryan.

Eventually, the third out was recorded. Grabbing my helmet, I took a deep breath and started towards the on-deck circle. Suddenly, a voice called from behind. It was Whitey's. "Johnny Mo, I know you haven't played in a while, so I figured I'd throw you in there against someone I know you can handle. Good luck." Whitey's bemusement could scarcely be hidden. I stepped into the batter's box and reminded myself to "attack the first good fastball." Ryan probably thought that coming off the bench I would be taking a pitch. I was determined to be ready in case he tried to sneak the first offering by me.

Ryan acknowledged the sign from batterymate Alan Ashby. He

began his delivery. I cocked my bat and shifted my weight back. Ryan let out his customary grunt as he released the ball. But this was not like any other pitch I had ever seen. The white pearl instantly became a blur, a 99 MPH heater coming directly at my head. As the ball buzzed past my ear I lost control of my body and wound up on my butt, flipped off my feet like a rag doll. How this heat-seeking missile missed splitting my head into thousands of tiny particles was a mystery to me. Only good reflexes and pure luck saved me from a trip to the hospital.

In a flash, I was on my feet. I would not give Ryan the satisfaction of thinking I was scared to death. But I was. I grabbed my bat off the ground and glanced towards the mound. There Ryan stood, glaring at me, with evil in his eyes. If this were a gunfight, then Ryan had Wyatt Earp down pat while I resembled a hapless Barney Fife. Ryan had scored early in this shootout with one strategically placed bullet, aimed at my head. Ryan's cold blank stare, his trademark for so many years, announced that he was all business.

I tried to conceal my fear of decapitation, but my shaking knees and the sweat pouring off my face were probably giving me away. As Ryan went into his delivery for the next pitch, I realized that I was scared blind. I barely caught a glimpse of another blazing fastball. It caught the outside corner. "Strike one!" the umpire yelled.

Ryan wasted little time after receiving the ball back from Ashby. He unleashed the next pitch at 96 MPH. As the ball painted the outside corner for strike two, I stood with the bat barely off my shoulder. Ryan had me pegged.

I stepped out of the box again, trying to collect myself. But I was a mess. I was no longer the cocky, confident batter who sat at the far end of the bench just minutes earlier. Instead, all I wanted was for this ordeal to end. I realized that the dugout was a much safer place. Ryan seemed poised, ready to finish me off.

The count was now one ball and two strikes. As I prepared for the next pitch I reminded myself to keep my head still. Maybe I was moving too much and that was causing me to not see the ball as clearly.

"Keep your head still. Just put the ball in play," I commanded my body as it shook violently in the batter's box. The once easy task of hitting a baseball, which I took for granted from the cozy confines of the dugout, had now become my worst nightmare. As each moment passed, mere contact mattered less and less. I just wanted to get out *alive*.

Ryan took the sign before unleashing another sizzling blur that painted the black on the outside corner. Once again, I watched it helplessly as the homeplate umpire hollered, "Strike three!"

The first at-bat of my career against the all-time strikeout king was now history. I could now be added to the list of hundreds of batters who had met a similar fate.

I walked back to the dugout with my head hanging low. After placing my bat in the rack I walked towards the end of the dugout with a glazed look on my face. The ever-jovial Whitey Herzog spoke up first. "Hey kid, if I'da been knocked on my ass the way you were, I'da done the same thing. Take three and get the hell out of town."

Laughter burst out around me as players and coaches had a good time at my expense. Tom Brunansky and Ken Dayley broke out in a chorus of Linda Rondstadt's "Blue Bayou" (or was it "Blew By You"?) I sat down next to Willie McGee and stared at my glove. Finally, I turned to Willie, shaking my head in disbelief. "How the hell does anybody hit that guy?" Willie started to laugh, probably recognizing my frazzled look from the faces of other young players who'd faced Ryan for the first time. McGee patted me on the back, paused for a moment, then asked me one simple question, "Looks a heck of a lot easier from over here, doesn't it"?

"Ted Williams is the man who always said that hitting a baseball was the toughest thing to do in sports. And I'm a disciple who says that hitting a baseball when you're coming off the bench, bottom of the ninth, against somebody throwing heat or split-fingered magic, is the toughest part of the toughest thing."

—Jay Johnstone

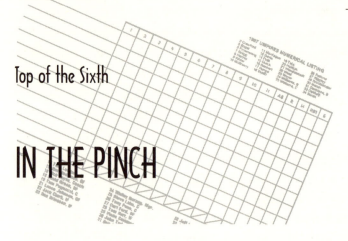

Top of the Sixth

IN THE PINCH

BASEBALL IS A GAME OF redemption. Go hitless today, and there is always tomorrow. Pinch hitters are denied that luxury. They don't revel in four at-bats a game, making adjustments along the way if necessary. They are baseball's lottery picks, bucking big odds in search of a payoff that rarely comes.

As the twists and turns of my career played out, I learned to not let the anxieties of pinch hitting get to me. My mentors turned out to be Hal McRae and Steve Braun, teammates who had immense success coming off the bench. Their advice helped me realize that mastery of the most difficult art of pinch hitting might be achieved through a properly laid-out plan of attack.

During the early 1980s, when I was a top prospect in the Kansas City Royals' organization, I often listened to McRae expound on the art of pinch hitting. McRae had a stellar 18-year career, six times batting over .300. Three times he made the All-Star team, and in 1982 he led the American League with 133 RBI. In 1985 McRae helped lead the Royals to a World Series Championship with his aggressive style of play

Hal McRae. (Photo courtesy of the National Baseball Hall of Fame Library, Cooperstown, NY)

95

and team-first spirit. The following season he set a Royals' record with a league-leading 15 pinch hits for a .319 batting average.

McRae was the full-time designated hitter for the Royals' championship teams of the 1970s and 1980s, and six times he was named the Designated Hitter of the Year by *The Sporting News.* When I first met him, as age and injury began to catch up with him, his playing time had decreased.

The first bit of advice McRae ever gave me about coming off the bench was: "If you just hit .200 as a pinch hitter, you're doing a helluva job." McRae realized that pinch hitters have the most difficult job in baseball, because they get one, and not four chances, to hit during a game. "Don't beat yourself up if you don't get the job done," he often said.

Victory and defeat are often determined in the late innings and the pressure on a pinch hitter can be overwhelming. McRae knew the odds were stacked against the hitter, so his advice to me was simple: "Don't think, you'll hurt the team. Just get a good pitch and knock the shit out of it."

Braun's career centered even more on pinch-hitting than McRae's. With 113 career pinch hits, Braun was one of the all-time greats. He piled up those hits in 402 at-bats for a .281 average. During one amazing stretch in the 1978 season with the Minnesota Twins, Braun reached base in 11 consecutive at bats. In 1986 we teamed together with Triple-A Louisville. He became my teacher and confidant, sharing countless hours addressing the subtle nuances of his craft. Braun was more analytical than McRae, and his success resulted because of the tremendous discipline he displayed at the plate. "Be selective," he often preached. "Remember, the pitcher is gonna give you at least one good pitch to hit. Don't do him a favor by just hacking at the first one that's close."

Braun's preparation emphasized a solid mental approach, and he continually reminded me to fill my mind with positive thoughts. For instance, if I had struck out as a pinch hitter, Braun encouraged me to find *something* positive about my effort. Maybe it would be the way I

Steve Braun. (Photo courtesy of the National Baseball Hall of Fame Library, Cooperstown, NY)

97

had battled with two strikes, or the way I had stayed back on a breaking ball. The idea was to eliminate any negative thoughts for the next at-bat. His strategy often worked. "Sometimes, you just have to trick your mind into thinking you're good," he noted. Braun also advised me to become a student of the game. "Pay attention to what's going on. Anticipate who you'll hit against late in the game. That way you'll never be surprised when Whitey calls on you."

Early in the 1989 spring training I found out all I wanted to know about Whitey calling on me. "Johnny, step into my office," he commanded one morning. "We need to talk."

"What's up?" I asked.

Whitey leaned back in his chair and brushed his fingers through his flattop. "Well, let me tell ya something, kid. I've had you now for three years, and I think I know you pretty damn well."

An internal alarm went off. "Oh shit," I thought. I already didn't like the direction this conversation might take, but I held my breath and let Whitey finish.

"To be perfectly honest with you, I think you do a hell of a lot more with one at-bat than you do with four."

Whitey's assessment had me scratching my head. Was I being patted on the back or kicked in the ass? I sensed it was latter and my hands began to sweat. He barked on. "When you pinch-hit, you really come off the bench swinging the stick. But sometimes I don't know what happens when you get four or five at-bats a game. I think maybe you put too much pressure on yourself."

I sank deeper in my chair. Whitey was on a roll. "When you start, I never know which hitter is gonna show up. The one who sometimes looks like Mickey Mantle, or the one who couldn't hit water if he fell out of a boat!"

Whitey's honesty, a trait I always admired, had left me dumbfounded. "As far as I'm concerned, kid, you're my guy off the bench. Just keep hackin', cause we're gonna need ya."

But I still wasn't sure how to react to this combination of praise and pep talk. I figured I didn't have room to complain. After all , I was play-ing in the major leagues for one of the most respected organizations in baseball. I lived in a great city and played in front of the most loyal fans in the game. And the pay wasn't bad either. So I signed on to this slightly redirected career path.

Once the regular season began I would arrive at the stadium each day by 2 P.M. so I'd have plenty of time to get ready for a 7:35 start. My daily routine included an hour of back exercises, a program that back surgery imposed on me following the 1987 season.

By 4 o'clock, I was taking my hacks on the Busch Stadium carpet under the watchful eye of batting instructor Johnny Lewis. My one chance to hit was still maybe five hours away. I would use this time to get into an aggressive state of mind. I would recall McRae's voice tell-ing me "expect the ball to be thrown exactly where you want it. And when you get that pitch, send it into next week."

After batting practice the preparation continued. On most days I buried myself in the video room and reviewed tape of my previous at-bats against that night's starter and all the righthanders in the bullpen. I focused my attention on how they attacked me. Maybe a certain pitcher would always start me off with breaking balls away. Or perhaps a pitcher tipped off his pitches with a glitch in his delivery. Whatever the case, I was in a neverending search for clues that would give me the upper hand.

Once the game began I would watch the first four innings from the bench. But as soon as the top of the fifth rolled around, it was off to the clubhouse for more stretching and a 10-minute ride on a sta-tionary bike.

By the sixth inning, I would have taken 30 swings off the batting tee. I used the long runway near the clubhouse to run sprints. And most importantly, I kept an eye on when our pitcher was scheduled to bat. All the possible pinch-hitting scenarios were already played out in my head. If our starter was pitching well and had the lead, he'd probably get to hit for himself in the fifth, sixth, or seventh inning. But if he was struggling and there was a chance for a rally, Whitey wouldn't hesitate to go to one of his "Bird Turds" in the pinch.

And so it was that the New York Mets came to town for the home opener of the season. David Cone, the Mets' starter and my former minor league teammate, cruised along as the Mets took a commanding lead into the late innings. I went into the outfield in the eighth inning and led off the home half of the ninth. Cone was regarded as one of the most aggressive pitchers in the league, and, true to form, he challenged me with his best stuff. After working the count to two balls and one strike, Cone came at me with another fastball. But this pitch, unlike the previous three offerings, was one I could handle. It was a flat, belt-high fastball that I crushed into the right-field seats for a home run. Though we lost the game, it was a good way to start the season in my first at-bat.

Several days later, my pinch-hit triple plated three runs against the Pirates. The following night, I pinch-hit in the ninth inning with the game on the line against the Montreal Expos. Tim Burke, the Expos' closer, was in the game. I knew him well, having played with him years earlier in winter ball. Since then, we had faced each other numerous times in both the minor and major leagues.

I knew he liked to start me off with sinkers away. "Make him get one up in the zone, out over the plate," I reminded myself as I sauntered to the plate. I didn't have to wait long. Burke's first pitch sinker turned into a floater. My eyes lit up and I unleashed a short, compact swing that sent a rising missile over the outstretched glove of shortstop Tom Foley for the game-winning knock.

For a bench guy, coming through in the pinch with the game on the line was the ultimate high.

In the first month of the campaign, which included a few starts in right field, I stroked 12 hits in 20 plate appearances for a mind-boggling .600 batting average. Even more impressive were the five pinch hits I collected in as many at-bats. I even became a factoid, complete with picture, in *USA Today*. I was in the proverbial "zone," the place a player gets to when everything becomes letter perfect. It's the time in a player's

TOP TEN

Player	Team	PA	AB	H	2B	3B	HR	RBI	BB	BA
John Morris	StL	13	12	5	2	1	0	5	1	.417
Carmelo Martinez	SD	11	9	3	1	0	0	1	2	.333
Curt Ford	Phi	17	17	5	0	0	0	1	0	.294
John Cangelosi	Pit	24	18	5	0	0	0	1	5	.278
Darrell Evans	Atl	11	11	3	0	0	0	0	0	.273
Dave Clark	Cle	10	8	2	0	0	1	2	2	.250
Greg Gross	Hou	10	8	2	0	0	0	1	2	.250
Ken Oberkfell	Pit-SF	12	12	3	1	0	0	3	0	.250
Bill Buckner	KC	12	12	3	0	0	0	0	0	.250
Lee Mazzilli	NYM	14	9	1	0	0	0	2	5	.222

BOTTOM TEN

Player	Team	PA	AB	H	2B	3B	HR	RBI	BB	BA
Craig Reynolds	Hou	11	11	0	0	0	0	0	0	.000
Gary Varsho	Cubs	15	15	1	0	0	0	0	0	.067
Geronimo Berroa	Atl	13	12	1	0	0	0	0	1	.083
John Moses	Min	10	10	1	0	1	0	2	0	.100
Dwayne Murphy	Phi	12	10	1	0	0	0	1	2	.100
Bob Dernier	Phi	10	10	1	0	0	0	0	0	.100
Dave Bergman	Det	10	9	1	0	0	0	0	1	.111
Franklin Stubbs	LA	10	9	1	0	0	0	0	1	.111
Gary Ward	NYY-Det	11	9	1	0	0	0	0	1	.111
Mike Aldrete	Mon	11	9	1	0	0	0	2	2	.111

Source: Project Scoresheet

Pinch Hitter Standings 1989

career when seemingly effortless results come about because the swing is short, the concentration focused, and the confidence is sky high.

But fame sometimes has a tendency to disappear in the blink of an eye.

The Cincinnati Reds came to town in the early part of May. Once again I wasn't in the starting lineup, but by now it didn't seem to matter. I figured finding a way to win the game in the late innings was a great way to spend a season.

On the first day of the series, the stage was set. I stepped to the plate in the ninth inning with the tying run on second base and two out. Rob Dibble, the Reds' fire-balling closer, had entered the game to extinguish the rally. His fastball was routinely clocked in the high 90s, and there were whispers around the league that he had recently registered triple digits on the radar gun. Not only could Dibble bring the

101

"high octane," but his herky-jerky, high leg kick hid the ball extremely well from the batter.

I had faced Dibble several times in Triple-A and the big leagues. Up to that point, he had the upper hand, but I was determined to get the better of him this time around.

Dibble's first pitch was some "low cheese" that caught the outside corner for strike one. His next pitch was a 99 MPH pellet. By the time I started my swing, the ball was already in Joe Oliver's mitt. Dibble was out for blood. He got the sign from Oliver and uncorked the sharpest slider I'd ever seen. But I was all over it. Or at least I thought so until I swung and missed it badly for strike three. The game was over, and so was my streak.

As I headed towards the clubhouse, a heckler with a Reds hat on his head and the remains of a 24-ounce beer in his hand gave me the business from behind our dugout. His slurred taunts caught my attention. After firing off a barrage of obscenities that would have made a sailor blush, he took one more gulp of brew and finished his tirade. "Hey, Morris, Dibble told me to remind you—That was good morning, good afternoon, and good night!"

Little did I realize that my appearance against Dibble would begin another streak, where I'd collect just one pinch hit over my next 15 appearances. Physically, I felt great. Mentally, my routine remained the same each day I came to the park. But there was one significant difference. Early in the season I had feasted on first-pitch fastballs. Advanced scouting reports now strongly suggested "don't start Morris off with hard stuff when he's coming off the bench. He'll hurt you."

During those 15 at-bats, I was served a steady diet of breaking balls and changeups. Now I was the one who had to make the adjustment. Patience would be a key if I were to get back on the right track. I had to continually remind myself of Braun's lessons on the subject. "Be patient," I could hear him say. "The pitcher will eventually give you a pitch you can handle."

By the time the season ended I averaged .220 as a pinch hitter, going 9-41. The nine hits could have easily been 13 or 14, but that's how the ball bounces sometimes in the life of a bench player.

That year, in a combination of only 25 starts, 71 late-game appearances, and 41 shots as a pinch hitter , I batted only 117 times, a small number considering I remained healthy the entire season. I finished at .239, but was proud I had come accumulated more than half of my hits as a non-starter.

At the ripe old age of 28, and in the prime of my baseball career, there was a part of me that felt I was too young to be a full-time pinch hitter. But because of the mental and physical challenges I faced each day and the immediate satisfaction that coming through could provide, I looked back on the season with pride.

Fans, friends, and family have often asked me what was the most difficult aspect of pinch hitting? At first I might offer them some gem I had picked up from McRae or Braun about aggressiveness or patience. But, in hindsight, I realized that the greatest challenge was actually the mere act of acceptance. Once upon a time I was an everyday player, luxuriating in four or five at-bats a game. Just letting go of that may have been the hardest part of it all.

"That's easy. Bob Gibson in 1968. The other four. Bob Gibson 1969, Bob Gibson 1970, Bob Gibson 1971, Bob Gibson 1972."
> —Doug Radar, asked to name the five toughest pitchers he ever encountered

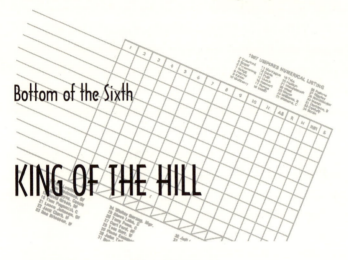

Bottom of the Sixth

KING OF THE HILL

AS THE ST. LOUIS SKIES opened up, a torrent of rain pelted the Busch Stadium Astroturf. The fifth inning had just ended when the downpour interrupted our game with the Atlanta Braves. With the precision of a surgical team, the 20-member grounds crew blanketed the field. Judging from the severity of the storm, it looked as if play would be delayed for a while.

With years of "rain delay" experience, several players quickly cranked up a variety of card games. Pitcher Ken Dayley dealt blackjack at one table while a game of Hearts grabbed the attention of another foursome. Some of the Redbirds listened to music on portable headsets, or milled around the room and answered fan mail as the rain delay approached an hour. A few just slumped in their seats and stared into their lockers.

Boredom had settled in, so I slid into the coaches' office and sat down next to hitting instructor Johnny Lewis. Six coaches, whose collective professional baseball experience exceeded 150 years, were engaged in a lively debate, comparing the talents of the modern-day ballplayer to players from generations past. Lewis was the first to pop off: "Years ago, there were more good hitters. I don't think today's players are as strong as the guys I played against."

Third-base coach Nick Leyva nodded in agreement, as did pitching coach Mike Roarke. I couldn't say I was surprised, given the fact that this crew of salty veterans had played in an era with names like Mantle, Mays, and Musial.

I took a stand for my contemporaries by firing back, "Sounds like sour grapes to me. I guess the next thing you're gonna tell me was that the pitching was also better back in the good old days." Red Schoendienst, the legendary Cardinals' coach and former skipper of the Redbirds during the 1960s and 1970s, chimed in from across the room, "That's exactly what I'm gonna tell you. Years ago when I managed, guys threw harder and had better control than most of today's pitchers."

I rolled my eyes to the ceiling and mumbled to myself, "Yeah right, Red. Do you want some cheese to go along with that whine?"

Red paused for a moment. "Oh, one more thing. The pitchers years ago were also tougher and nastier. And just in case you don't believe me, try asking the guy sitting beside you."

I snapped my head to the right. There sat Bob Gibson, the most successful pitcher to ever wear a Cardinals' uniform. Gibson sat quietly with his legs crossed and his hands cupped on his lap.

During the rain delay Bob had made his way down to the clubhouse from the KMOX radio booth where he had been a broadcaster for the St. Louis station the previous three seasons. After a brilliant Hall-of-Fame career with the Cards, and several stints as a major league pitching coach, Bob had made a smooth transition from superstar baseball player to media personality.

I studied Gibson, and I couldn't help but admire the tremendous poise and tranquility of a man many baseball experts, including the Cardinals' coaching staff, considered to be one of the most competitive and intense pitchers of all-time.

Bob Gibson. (Photo courtesy of the National Baseball Hall of Fame Library, Cooperstown, NY)

During my first three years playing in St. Louis I had learned about the championship Cardinals teams from years past. During the 1960s and 1970s, when power pitchers ruled the game, few were as dominant as Bob Gibson. Among the most successful of World Series performers, Gibson won 251 games, compiled an ERA of 2.91, and struck out 3,117 batters during his 17-year career.

Born in 1935 in Omaha, Nebraska, Gibson grew up an outstanding athlete and played basketball with the world famous Harlem Globetrotters before signing a contract with the Cards in 1957. By 1963, he was the ace of the staff and the following year he led the Cards to a World Series championship. In 1968, Gibson won both the MVP and Cy Young Award. His 22-9 record and league-best 268 strikeouts were actually outshined by an all-time low ERA of 1.12 and 13 shutouts. Tim McCarver, current baseball broadcaster and former batterymate for Gibson during the 1960s, had an interesting insight about Gibson during the 1968 campaign: "Bob Gibson is the luckiest pitcher I ever saw. He always pitched when the other team didn't score any runs."

Gibson's displayed remarkable athletic ability throughout his career as he smacked 24 lifetime home runs and won nine consecutive Gold Gloves.

Pride also played a huge role in Gibson's character and success. As with other African-American players, he had been forced to stay in a private home during spring training in 1958 because hotels in St. Petersburg, Florida, had prohibited blacks from occupying rooms. The struggle to overcome racism was something Gibson dealt with throughout his career. By the early 1960s Gibson was one of the pioneers who helped force Florida hotels to finally accept blacks.

With the pause in the conversation beginning to lengthen, I swallowed hard and struggled to find something intelligent to say. Our paths had crossed many times in my first three years with the Cards and rarely had I ever gotten anything more than a passing nod. I figured that Gibson was either a very shy man or, as some legends had it, a brooding maniac.

Coach Dave Ricketts called from a nearby cubicle, "On the days Gibson pitched, he was the meanest S.O.B. you'd ever want to meet. Not only did he hate the opposition, he wouldn't even speak to his own teammates when he pitched. And God forbid he ever caught one of his teammates talking to the other team; Gibson would pinch that poor sucker's head off."

I suspected Ricketts was right ,but I needed confirmation. "Is that true, Bob?"

Gibson sat in stony silence for several seconds before he began to laugh. "Yeah, I guess so."

Pitching coach Mike Roarke glanced up from his *New York Times* crossword puzzle to throw in his two cents. "Hey, Johnny Mo, Gibby would drill his mother in the ribs with a fastball if he thought it would help him win a game."

"No way," I said, shaking my head.

Over the next 10 minutes, the stories about Mr. Bob Gibson's legend continued. But Gibson himself tortured me with silence as he continued to reveal absolutely nothing about himself.

Finally, I made my move. Here was my golden opportunity to strike up a conversation with the man who hadn't said "boo" to me in four years.

Fidgeting a little I cleared my throat. "Bob, do me a favor. Tell me just one story that supports what these guys are saying about you."

Suddenly, Gibson perked up. "Well, let's see," he started. "I was pitching in 1968 against the Dodgers."

Foolishly, I interrupted, "That was the year you had the 1.12 ERA, right?"

Gibson gave me the evil eye. "Umm, yeah that's right. Anyway, where was I?"

Ricketts fired away from across the room, "Morris, shut the hell up and let Gibson tell the story." My face flushed with embarrassment so I resolved to tighten my lip.

Gibson picked up the story. His eyes brightened and he sat up straight in his chair. "So we're playing the Dodgers, and this young Latin kid I'd never seen before leads off the game."

I wanted to know the player's name, but I kept quiet to avoid embarrassing myself again. Relief came as Gibson, now more animated, continued. "I can't remember the kid's name. Some little Punch and Judy rookie from the Dominican Republic. So this kid leads off the game and I throw him a first pitch fastball, which he bunts perfectly down the third-base side for a hit."

Coach Leyva shook his head. "That kid had a huge set of brass balls if you ask me."

"Well, now I know the kid can bunt," said Gibson. "So, the kid comes up again in the bottom of the third inning with two out and a runner on first."

Off to the side Coach Roarke put down his crossword puzzle and Coach Hacker stuffed his copy of *Golf Digest* back in his locker. Half a dozen pair of eyes were now riveted on Gibson.

He was on a roll. "I still didn't know much about this kid, so I threw him another fastball right down the middle. I couldn't believe it but the kid bunted again. This time he dragged the ball past me on the first-base side. By the time I picked up the ball the damn kid was already past first base."

"I remember that, Gibby," chuckled Red Schoedienst. "I was sitting in the dugout laughing my ass off after that kid dropped that second bunt on you."

"I'm glad you were amused, Red" snapped Gibson.

Coach Hacker chirped in from the far end of the room, "I'm afraid to ask what happened next."

I could see the juices rising in Gibson's body as he gathered steam. His lips tightened and the veins in his neck grew large.

"So this kid comes up again in the fifth inning with two outs and nobody on. Hell would freeze over before I was going to let him bunt again."

I suspected what was coming next. I figured Gibson would brush the kid back off the plate with a fastball. Or maybe he would start him off with a first-pitch breaking ball.

Gibson was now like a runaway freight train. "So this kid digs into the batter's box. McCarver gave me the sign for a curveball and I shook him off because I wanted to throw another fastball. I wound up and threw a heater, and ya know what happened next?"

The entire room held its collective breath as Gibson delivered the final blow. "I drilled the kid right in the frickin head!"

My mouth opened wide and the hair on the back of my neck stood straight up. I asked the first thing that came to mind, "What did you do next?"

Gibson fired back, "Well, I walked towards homeplate and picked the ball up off the ground. It looked like the kid was in La-La Land."

"Did you say anything to him" I asked.

"Oh yeah, I stood over him, looked him straight in the eyes and said, *"Bunt that, asshole!"*

The coaches let out a collective roar. I, on the other hand, was stunned by Gibson's indifference to the near decapitation of the Dodger rookie.

Ozzie Smith beckoned me back into the clubhouse, and by the time I returned to the coaches' room, Gibson was gone. The game was getting ready to resume, so I figured he had returned to the radio booth.

After a 90-minute rain delay we were back on the field. About 45 minutes later, I batted against Paul Assenmacher in the bottom of the seventh inning.

The veteran lefthander started me off with a fastball that drilled me on the back of my arm. I walked slowly to first base while Gibson's story bounced around my head.

As I stood on the bag, rubbing the tender part of my tricep, I snuck a glance up towards the radio box where Bob Gibson sat. Although I couldn't see his face, I imagined him sitting in his chair high above the action with a look of satisfaction on his face.

"The clubhouse is one of the seductions of baseball; it is a place where you don't have to grow up."

—Reggie Jackson

Top of the Seventh

THREE-MAN DEAD LIFT

BASEBALL WAS IN THE MIDST of a serious crisis during the winter of 1990. In a bitter dispute over a new labor agreement, owners of baseball teams were preparing to "lock out" the players. Verbal hand grenades were launched across the negotiating table as a battle between team owners and the Major League Baseball Players Association threatened the start of spring training and the regular season.

Spring training traditionally opens in mid-February in various cities throughout Arizona and Florida. Optimism usually reigns, as players dream about making it to the World Series in October. But this was no ordinary spring training. The owners had taken a hard line with the players' union, and the impasse forced all of the training facilities to shut down for several weeks. Finally, in early March, the two parties reached an agreement. Although the players were permitted to return to work, animosity between owners and players remained dangerously high. It was under this cloud of bitterness, mistrust, and suspicion that spring training finally began in mid-March.

A lot of new faces were present in the Cardinals' camp that spring, many I had never met before. Yet the determined look in their eyes suggested they were eager and ready to go. One player in particular made quite an impression on the entire team. His name was Howard Hilton, a right-handed pitcher who had played Double-A ball in Arkansas the year before.

Howard stood 6'3" and weighed a hefty 260 pounds. His physical condition left much to be desired. Simply stated, Howard Hilton was a *very* large man. His flabby belly hung over his belt and his puffy cheeks made his face seem enormous. Howard's huge back caused the numbers and letters on his uniform jersey to stretch widely across his torso. This was topped off by a closely cropped crew cut, with each strand of hair standing straight up.

Appearing in his first major league camp, Howard was not like most rookies out to make a good impression. His work ethic was not ideal for a professional athlete. Grossly out of shape, he showed little interest in improving his exercise regimen or his diet. But Howard was not being defiant—he was just being Howard. Every morning, he ambled into the clubhouse with a fresh bag of donuts. Like a shark attacking a school of fish, Howard would consume the contents of the bag within minutes.

Food was in abundance around the clubhouse and Howard was a pro at inhaling his fair share. And his ability to consume massive quantities of beer made him the ideal couch potato. On top of this, Howard was a master at doing the minimal amount of physical and aerobic activity. Extra wind sprints, forget it. Sit ups, are you kidding? Lazy, undisciplined, and unmotivated—that was Howard all the way.

But the big kid from Northern California sure could pitch. Once he set foot on the mound he transformed into a fierce competitor who loved going after hitters. He attacked his opponents with the same gusto he tackled a post-game spread.

During the previous season, Howard had recorded more than 20 saves. He was the best pitcher on the team, possessing a lively fastball that regularly exceeded 90 MPH. His repertoire also included a hard-biting slider and a split-fingered fastball that made hitters look foolish

Howard Hilton (Photo © St. Louis Baseball Cardinals)

when they swung at it. Howard possessed an upbeat, positive attitude that served him well whenever he pitched, especially in pressure situations. Load the bases, and Howard would happily work his way out of the jam. Knock him around with a few line drives and Howard would keep on going after the hitters.

Howard was also blessed with the gift of gab. He could easily strike up a conversation with anybody. It didn't matter if it was an eight-year-old kid, or manager Whitey Herzog. He often had a great deal to say and rarely hesitated to voice his opinion. His booming voice could get the attention of anybody within earshot. But his opinions were never mean spirited or nasty. He was essentially as harmless as a big teddy bear.

Unfortunately, Howard's introduction to major league baseball came at a time when it was better for rookies to be seen and not heard. He frequently made the mistake of speaking too often in front of veteran teammates, and was consistently putting not one, but both feet in his mouth. But Howard's charming innocence helped him get out of these holes. You couldn't help but like him.

As we approached the final days of spring training, it appeared that Howard was going to make the team. He was pitching well, showing improvement with each outing. For the most part, his sinking fastball and wicked slider stunned the competition. As his on-field performance improved, his impromptu clubhouse acts became more frequent. Howard seemed to be enjoying himself immensely. After each game he held verbal court in the center of the clubhouse, sharing his excitement with anyone who had enough patience to endure his persistent rambling.

With a week left in spring training, several players decided that Howard Hilton needed to have some of the air let out of his balloon. Enter Tom Brunansky, outfielder and one of the team's unofficial pranksters. Also known as "Bruno," Tom came up with a brilliant idea: he would ask Howard to participate in an event known as the "Three-Man Dead Lift."

I was chosen as the point man to lure Howard in, and struck up a supposedly innocent conversation with him about the "Lift." I explained that Brunansky owned the major league baseball record for lifting 750 pounds off the ground, having shattered the old mark of 700 pounds with relative ease. I told him how Bruno was out to break his own mark, and how difficult it would be to execute. By the end of my rambling explanation, it was clear to me that Howard wanted to be part of the record-breaking attempt.

To perform the "Lift" Bruno needed three large teammates. Joe Magrane and Danny Cox, each weighing 250 pounds, volunteered to assist. Bruno then approached all 260 pounds of Howard, indicating that he was the key to achieving the next milestone.

"Howard," said Bruno, "we need you to be part of the 'Three-Man Dead Lift.' What do ya say?"

The words were barely out of Bruno's mouth when Howard said, "Count me in. Besides, I don't think you can do it. I have to see this for myself."

I began promoting the "Three-Man Dead Lift" in earnest. For two days, I whipped the team into a frenzy about how Bruno was going to dismantle his own record. Aside from being chief promoter, I was also the official bookmaker. Bets came flying at me from every direction. Ozzie Smith and Vince Coleman waved $100 bills in the air, certain that Bruno would fail. Other players, including Terry Pendleton and Ken Dayley, bet their money on Bruno.

The stage was set. Bruno announced that tomorrow morning he would make weightlifting history. And Howard let everyone know that he would be there bright and early. "I wouldn't miss this for the world," he said. "Bruno's got no chance of lifting the three of us off the ground." Many of us could see Howard giggling to himself as he left the clubhouse for the day.

The following morning at exactly 9 A.M., Bruno entered the clubhouse, beaming with confidence and looking ready to lift a building. His white tank top displayed his well-defined shoulders and biceps, his weight belt strapped tight around his waist.

Tony Peña, our starting catcher, began hollering in his Latin accent, "I say 500 dollar Bruno no can get the three amigos off the ground."

From the other side of the clubhouse, pitcher Bob Forsch shouted, "I'll take that bet, Peña! Five-hundred dollars says Bruno breaks the record!"

For the next five minutes, pandemonium filled the room as players and coaches waved money at each other with wagers exceeding $2,000. The atmosphere was electric, and Howard Hilton was right in the center of it.

Bruno made his way towards the center of the room, barking instructions to Magrane, Cox, and Hilton. "OK, I need all three of you on the floor. Magrane, you on one side; Cox, you on the other. I want Hilton in the center because he's the heaviest. This way the weight will be evenly distributed."

Before Howard lay down on the floor, he pulled me off to the side of the room. "Johnny Mo," he whispered, "I need a favor. I want you to bet an extra fifty bucks for me *against* Bruno." He smiled as he handed me the money, a devilish look plastered on his face. "I promise you, he'll never get me off the ground. Look here, I've added five-pound weights to my pockets. He's got no chance. Just keep this between me and you."

Howard wasn't kidding. There they were, two round discs stuffed in the pockets of his home uniform whites, each weighing five pounds. Howard had sunk to an all-time low, obviously willing to do anything to keep Bruno from breaking his own record.

Howard slid onto the floor. His huge torso wedged between Magrane and Cox. Their combined weight was now 770 pounds—including the additional 10 pounds Howard had snuck into his pants.

The key to Bruno's success depended largely on having the three players tightly interlocked. Their legs had to be bound like pretzels— their arms tightly fitted around each other's necks. Bruno expertly directed the players in positioning their bodies perfectly. And Howard Hilton was the centerpiece, the anchor, and the foundation. He wasn't going anywhere, incapable of doing anything other than breathing. The three of them might as well have been glued to each other—one solid mass of humanity.

Bruno issued final instructions by reminding the threesome to squeeze as hard as possible when he told them to. The room became quiet as Bruno began deep breathing, his eyes closed as if he were meditating. While he was breathing, many of the players quietly and unexpectedly left the room.

Bruno opened his eyes and looked down at the three tangled players. "Okay," he said, "when I count to three I need all of you to tighten your bodies for as long as possible." Magrane and Cox nodded their heads in agreement. Howard had a confident look on his face; one that suggested he was about to become 50 bucks richer. Bruno took three quick, deep breaths, taking in as much oxygen as his lungs could hold. "Here we go gentlemen, one, two, three, now!"

Magrane, Cox, and Hilton tightened their bodies as they held their collective breath. Their grip was devastating. Howard's face became flushed and his eyes closed. Veins stood out from his neck. Grunting and groaning noises filled the air.

Bruno reached down and grabbed the belt on Howard's size 42 uniform pants. Suddenly, seemingly out of nowhere, a herd of screaming players charged into the room. The noise was deafening as the group headed directly at Bruno and the threesome. Taking his cue from the charging mob, Bruno let go of Howard's belt, turned, and slid out the clubhouse door with a silly grin on his face.

The pack of players, led by Vince Coleman and Terry Pendleton, pounced on the tangled threesome, but they focused on one person and one person only—Howard Hilton. The players were armed with an assortment of goodies—shaving cream, shampoo, baby oil, peanut butter, and baby powder—just to name a few.

Howard struggled violently to free himself from the tangled web created by Joe Magrane and Danny Cox. But the two bookends displayed Superman-like strength as Howard twisted his body in a vain effort to reach freedom.

117

Tony Peña was at the head of the pack. He reached down and un-buttoned Howard's pants, exposing his size 42 Fruit of the Looms to the room. For the next two minutes, the mob emptied their items onto Howard Hilton's massive frame. They stuffed mounds of peanut butter down his pants. They covered his head and face with shaving cream, shampoo, chocolate syrup, and baby powder. By the time the damage was complete, Howard was covered from head to toe.

Howard eventually surrendered and his body went limp. Once he stopped fighting, Magrane and Cox relinquished their tenacious grip and rolled away, each with satisfied grins on their faces. Their bodies were completely unmarked; a sign that the intended target had been hit with great accuracy.

Howard lay motionless on the floor, his face an unrecognizable mess, chocolate syrup oozing off his body. The scent of lemon shaving creme mixed with peanut butter wafted through the room. The demolition and humiliation of Howard Hilton was complete, performed with surgeon-like precision and efficiency.

The clubhouse filled with laughter once again. Players, coaches, trainers, and media personnel had now witnessed the setup and execution of the infamous "Three-Man Dead Lift" against Howard Hilton. Bruno had given a masterful performance and he now received the hearty congratulations from his teammates with grace and humor.

Tony Peña and other players danced around the room like little kids as the celebration continued for several more minutes. The mood in the room was festive, the team's energy level the highest it had been all spring. All the while, Howard Hilton remained on the floor in silence, speechless for the first time since we'd known him. The dazed look on his messy face, bringing tears of laughter to his hysterical teammates.

Minutes later, I made my way to the bathroom area of the club-house. My sides were hurting from laughing so hard. As I stood over the sink washing my hands, a noise from behind startled me. It was Howard, looking like the featured creature from a grade B horror flick. He was anxious to remove the cremes, soaps, gels, and other assorted crap from his body.

Suddenly, he glanced at me, a hint of embarrassment etched on his face. I was standing in front of the showers, trapped, with nowhere to go. Howard looked me in the eye as he calmly slid off his uniform pants and dropped them on the floor. He seemed to have something hidden in his massive hands.

I sensed I was in trouble as he quickly approached and cut down the distance between us. When he got within five feet of me, he suddenly raised both arms as if he was going to hit me. In a flash, I realized that Howard probably thought I was the mastermind behind the prank, and he was out for revenge.

"Morris," he said grimly, "I've got something I want to say to you."

My knees felt weak and I began to tremble. I swallowed hard before asking, "What's that, buddy?"

He opened his hands, displaying the two five-pound weights. "I guess I won't be needing these after all," he said, a grin spreading across his face.

Instant relief.

The two of us burst into laughter as my fear of Howard vanished.

Over the remaining days of spring training, Howard Hilton mellowed a great deal. Perhaps a bit gun-shy, he was not nearly as boisterous as he had been the first few weeks. He began to display a calmness and humility that was appealing. He was much more subdued around the veteran players, maybe realizing that a rookie is indeed better off being seen and not heard.

With opening day just a few days away, Whitey Herzog informed Howard that he had made the team, and would be heading north with the parent club.

For the first month of the season, Howard pitched in several games. His results were mixed, like those of most rookies barging onto the major league scene for the first time. On occasion he overwhelmed his opponents; other times, he was pounded into submission. But despite the outcome, one thing remained constant—Howard's attitude. He continued to carry himself in the same playful manner as he did during

Top of the Seventh

spring training. Day in and day out, he was having the time of his life.

As the season entered the first week of May, the team needed to make several roster moves. One of the players reassigned to the minor leagues was Howard Hilton. He would spend the remainder of the season with the Triple-A team. Unfortunately, that was the last time Howard Hilton ever wore a major league uniform. Howard remained a member of the Cardinals' organization for the next two years before gaining his release.

Howard Hilton will not be remembered as the greatest pitcher of all time. But Howard did make a great contribution to the Cardinals' organization and to baseball during the tenuous 1990 baseball season. At a time when major league baseball was riddled with serious problems and its outlook was grim, Howard popped onto the scene. He made the environment in the clubhouse light, entertaining, and amusing. He provided everyone with an opportunity to view baseball the way it was supposed to be—a game enjoyed by those who play it well.

"If the human body recognized agony and frustration, people would never run marathons, have babies, or play baseball."

—Carlton Fisk

Bottom of the Seventh

MY ACHING BACK

LIFE WAS VERY GOOD. In June 1990, I had been in the "bigs" already for four years and I had just gotten engaged to Linda. I pulled a left off of Spruce Street into the Busch Stadium parking lot and waved my usual "hello" to the attendant. I wheeled into my favorite spot right next to Ozzie Smith's Mercedes. I got out and slammed the door on my Blazer within a minute of my usual 2 o'clock arrival time.

Suddenly, with the surety of a sniper's bullet, a white-hot bolt of lower back pain dropped me to my knees. Through the excruciating agony I could make out the thought "I'm in deep trouble." Trying to gather my senses I hauled myself up to a standing position and began staggering to the clubhouse.

The usual five-minute stroll turned into a 20-minute nightmare as stabbing pain plagued my every step. Once inside, I slowly dressed myself hoping no one would notice my condition. For the first time I was relieved to know I wasn't in the starting lineup that evening against the Philadelphia Phillies, but I realized it was only a matter of time before Whitey discovered I had blown my back out—again.

My back had betrayed me once before, but this was without a doubt the worst pain I'd ever experienced. I'd had back problems three years earlier during the 1987 season, but had put off doing anything about it until after our World Series against the Minnesota Twins. In early November I was told I had two ruptured discs in my back. So I decided to have surgery, confident that it would alleviate my pain and suffering. Following the operation, I adopted a grueling back stabilization program, designed to strengthen the major muscle groups surrounding my fragile spine. The program became as important to my survival as eating, sleeping, and breathing. For two years it had worked wonders. I would count on it again to save my baseball career.

But first I had to make it through this game.

I hid at the far end of the dugout hoping Whitey would forget I ever existed. But in the seventh inning my luck ran out. "Johnny, go to right field," he barked. I nervously fumbled for my glove and hobbled to my position, praying the ball would be hit to someone else.

My prayer went unanswered. Pinch hitter Ron Jones drilled the first pitch of the inning into the right-field corner. My instincts took over and I made a move after the ball with a tentative first step. A split second later a paralyzing sensation grabbed hold of my body. My legs were betraying me, but somehow I managed to drag myself to the ball without falling flat on my face. I scooped it up and threw it towards the infield as if I were launching a grenade, secretly hoping that none of the 35,000 fans noticed my condition. I felt helpless, wondering how I would survive what now felt like the longest inning of my life.

After the third out was recorded, I hauled my body off the field. I knew I couldn't continue playing. Third baseman Terry Pendleton caught me as I fell down from the top of the dugout steps. In a flash, he whisked me through a long dark tunnel that led to the training room. Within minutes, team physician Stan London hovered above me. The concern in his eyes confirmed that I was seriously injured.

Hours later, Willie McGee dropped me off at my apartment, where I spent the night wondering what kind of freight train had run over me.

But at least for one evening, massive doses of painkillers did their prescribed job. Over the next week, I limped around as cortisone pills and muscle relaxers did little to stem the pain flaming away in my back and shooting down my legs.

As the pain intensified, my emotional state of mind became a cause for concern. I spent countless hours barricaded inside my apartment in an effort to avoid friends, fans, and teammates. The last thing I wanted was for another sympathetic soul asking me "How's your back doing?" or "When are you gonna be able to play again?" Addressing people's questions and concerns only made me more depressed. Although I did a masterful job avoiding everybody, I couldn't escape the dangerous conversation that pounded off the walls of my head. My persistent thoughts conjured up images of a future consumed by chronic pain and bitterness at having to retire from baseball because of a career-ending injury.

Finally I snapped out of my funk. Instead of waiting for a miracle to occur, I boarded a plane to Los Angeles and sought the advice of Dr. Robert Watkins. Recognized as the top back specialist in the country, Watkins was the surgeon who recommended the back stabilization program after my first surgery. I had tremendous confidence in his abilities.

After his initial exam, nurses ushered me around the hospital for a battery of tests, including MRIs and CAT scans. Within an hour, the test results confirmed my worst nightmare—another herniated disc. In addition, scar tissue had wrapped itself around a nerve root, causing the burning sensation in my legs and feet. It didn't take long to figure out my options were limited. I could try to strengthen the area around the spine by continuing the trunk stabilization program, or undergo surgery number two. I decided to take Dr. Watkins' advice and rehab my back for a month before I would consider another surgery. But after four grueling weeks of stretching, strengthening, and aerobic conditioning I was no better off. Despite being able to perform my daily regimen I was still in so much pain that performing any baseball-related activities was out of the question.

123

Frustration and anxiety finally got the best of me and so I opted to go back under the knife. But this time I was more confident about the outcome, knowing that the premiere back specialist in the United States was in charge.

Following surgery in August, Watkins suggested my problem was fixed. He even recommended I begin the back program as soon as I returned home to Florida. It was the best news I had received in a long time. Convinced my problems were finally behind me, I greeted the rehab with renewed enthusiasm and determination. I knew that the three hours of daily therapy would move me closer to playing baseball again. In addition, an hour-long aerobics program was added to help me regain strength and stamina. I knew that in order to make it back to the playing field I would have to work harder than ever before in my life.

Besides the physical challenges I faced, I also had several issues that needed to be addressed with the front office. So with only days remaining in the season, I paid a visit to Dal Maxvill, general manager of the Cardinals. I was anxious to find out if he could shed some light on my future with the team.

Several days prior to the All-Star break in July, shock waves had hit the Cardinals' organization when Whitey Herzog resigned as manager. Our season had turned into a major disappointment, and Joe Torre, a former star with the Cardinals during the 1970s, was handed the managerial reins. Torre had previously piloted the New York Mets and Atlanta Braves, and he appeared ready to get the Cards headed back in the right direction.

Torre's appointment as manager also signaled that a rebuilding process within the organization was under way. Top minor prospects were getting a chance to make their mark. Our most popular player, Willie McGee, had been traded for more prospects. Injured and unable to play since Torre took over, I assumed I couldn't possibly be in his future plans. I couldn't blame him for moving forward without me.

As my meeting with Maxvill unfolded I realized my days with the Cardinals were numbered. I fidgeted in my chair and listened to

Maxvill gush about the up-and-coming stars in the minor league system. By the time the meeting ended, I had wangled an invitation to spring training, but no contract offer. It was not exactly a ringing endorsement. I figured Maxvill probably wanted to see if my newly repaired back could withstand the rigors of playing every day before he would ask for my John Hancock on a contract.

As I stood to leave I turned towards Maxvill to ask a question that had been haunting me for some time. "Hey, Dal," I started, "has there ever been any talk about replacing the Astroturf with real grass?" Artificial turf had for many years been the Busch Stadium playing surface. Many baseball owners liked the "green concrete" because it greatly reduced the possibility of rain delays, cancellations, and most importantly, lost revenue. Even if it stormed all day in St. Louis, the field could be ready 30 minutes after the rain stopped.

Unfortunately, Astroturf had also been blamed for many injuries. For years, players had complained about pain in their feet, legs, knees, and backs. I was convinced that playing on it for several years had contributed greatly to my own physical problems.

Maxvill replied, "John, we have fans driving from Arkansas, Oklahoma, Illinois, and Kansas. If it rains, we don't want them going home because the field is unplayable."

"But what about what's best for the players?" I asked.

Maxvill scoffed, "A wise man once told me something very interesting." He took a deep breath before continuing. "He said that the rancher will always be there—he'll just go out and get new cattle."

Shock quickly turned to anger. I stormed out of his office convinced that baseball's stuffed shirts cared only about one thing—the almighty dollar.

In my heart I knew it was time to move on. I would be a free agent in a few weeks anyway. But would another team gamble on a broken down 30-year-old major leaguer with two back surgeries on his medical resume?

Several days after that meeting from hell, disaster struck again. One day while dressing I noticed that my lower back had become swollen, inflamed, and hot to the touch. I would soon find out that I had become the victim of a nasty infection that had worked its way to the base of my spinal canal.

For the next two weeks, bouts of fatigue and nausea gripped me like a vice. My skin turned yellow, and it was a struggle to stay awake for more than two hours at a time. Prescription drugs did little to help. On four occasions I dragged my body into the doctor's office to have the puffy mass drained from my back. Each time the doctor would relieve the pressure, but within 24 hours the infection would return.

Although I had barely noticed, the season had ended, and I continued to feel lousy. Even Linda was having a hard time hiding her concern. Depression had another hold on me, and it got worse with each passing day. One evening after my shower, my towel became covered with a thick yellow liquid. Horrified, I turned to face the bathroom mirror only to see that the hot water had ripped open a baseball-sized hole in my back. My stomach did a flip at the sight of it. I managed to patch the area back together with gauze pads and medical tape and within 24 hours I had flown back to Dr. Watkins' Los Angeles office again.

It didn't take more than a few minutes for Watkins to give me the bad news. "I'm admitting you to the hospital immediately. The infection in your back needs to be removed as soon as possible."

I was shocked. "I thought last month's operation fixed my problem. How could this happen?"

"Unfortunately," Watkins replied, "the chance of infection increases significantly after any second operation. I'm hopeful the infection didn't enter your spinal canal. Another operation is the only way to keep you from getting a lot sicker than you already are."

I lay motionless on the table. I began to think of all the horrible things that could happen to me if another surgery failed. Would I ever walk again? Or worse, could this infection wind up in my brain and kill me?

Finally, I snapped out of my panic. "So what's next?"

"After the surgery, you'll receive intravenous antibiotic treatments three times a day, every day, for six weeks," said Watkins. "That is the only way to be sure the infection is no longer a threat to your health."

The following morning I was back on the operating table. Watkins performed his second surgery on me in six weeks and I awoke that afternoon stretched out on my stomach. It was a strange feeling, one that I would have to endure for the next three days so the hole in my back would begin to heal properly.

After a week in the hospital I returned home to Florida with a fresh pink scar on my back and 15 pounds missing from my once solid frame.

Three times a day Linda helped me administer the daily intravenous treatments. But the next six weeks added bounce to my step and a sparkle to my eyes. By the time the treatments were complete I began, for the first time in a very long time, having thoughts of playing baseball again.

With spring training still three months away, I began to contact general managers and farm directors from a dozen teams, hoping somebody would take a chance on me. Fortunately, one of those was Lee Thomas, general manager of the Phillies. Though keenly aware of my medical situation, he was still willing to offer me a ray of hope. He proved it by inviting me to major league camp.

With the physical and mental trauma I had encountered over the previous months I was unsure how much more baseball my body could withstand. But if I were going to be forced into retirement, I was determined to go down fighting. In early January I began to workout with "Hap" Hudson, strength and conditioning coach for the Phillies. Hap had been my trainer when I played Triple-A ball with Louisville in 1985 and 1986. His tireless work ethic and positive attitude were attributes I greatly admired. Hap became my therapist, trainer, psychologist, and drill sergeant. Each day Hap had me run wind sprints, lift weights, and stay on my back program with a laser sharp focus. He even put me through two challenging 45-minute aerobic workouts each day so I'd be able to withstand the long hours on my feet once spring training began. By the middle of February I had whipped my

127

body into the best physical condition of my life. Even the lost weight, once a cause for concern, would become an advantage as it relieved pressure off my back.

On February 20, 1991, eight months and two more surgeries after my terrifying episode in the Busch Stadium parking garage I was back on a baseball field. On the first day of spring training in Clearwater, Florida, I didn't need to remind myself how fortunate I was to be back playing baseball.

However, joy and pride hid a tremendous fear of re-injury. There was a new challenge being issued. I was about to find out if I could make it back to "the show."

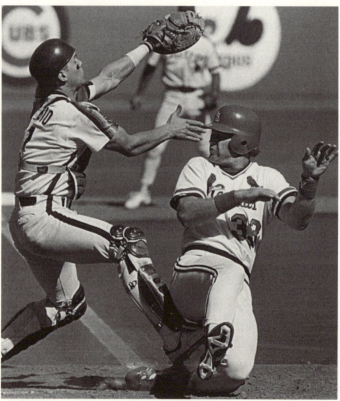

Weeks prior to injuring my back again. Avoiding the tag of friend and former Seton Hall standout, Craig Biggio of the Astros. (Photo by Ted Reisinger)

"Because of the length of the season, humor plays a big role in baseball. It's also important to know when the proper time is for humor. Roger had a great feel for when to use it, and when not to use it."

—John Vukovich

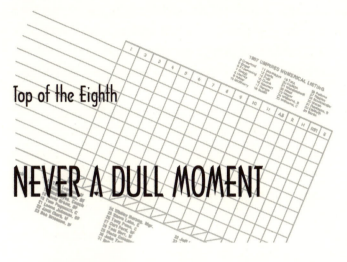

Top of the Eighth

NEVER A DULL MOMENT

"OH DAMN!"

With my jockey shorts stretched around my ankles and a sports section sitting on my lap, I flinched as the firecracker landed, sizzling just a yard away from my feet.

Ka-boom!

"What the hell's going on?" I screamed once the ring in my ears stopped.

"Sorry about that, Mo," howled Roger McDowell from the bathroom entrance. "I was just trying to kill this cockroach in the sink."

Only days into the 1991 spring training, the clown prince of the Philadelphia Phillies, the premiere practical joker in all of major league baseball, was up to his old tricks.

"Have a nice day," laughed Roger as his voice trailed off into the clubhouse. From that moment on, taking a seat on the toilet with Roger anywhere in the same area code was sure to be a nail-biting experience.

Of course, this was not Roger's first attempt at pyrotechnical expertise. Actually, he had apprenticed in his use of explosives in his early days as a relief pitcher with the New York Mets. I would now get an inside look at Roger's twisted sense of humor as we joined forces in the "City of Brotherly Love."

Early in the regular season, my former team, the Cardinals, flew into town for a three-game series. In the first inning of the first game, Roger sat patiently in the dugout with a mischievous grin on his face—the same look that masks a kid's face when he knows he's about to do something wrong. I sat nearby, and I watched him finesse a book of matches, a cigarette, and a wad of bubble gum in his fingers.

"Hey, what's up?" I asked.

"Relax," whispered Roger, "gimme a minute and you can see for yourself."

His nimble fingers wrapped the gum around the cigarette and the matches. Once certain all the parts were in good working order, Roger then cupped the device in his hands behind his head, leaned back, and waited for the third out to be recorded.

Moments later the inning ended, and as our team hustled off the field Roger slid into position. Cardinals starter Bryn Smith then began taking his warm-up tosses while our first-base coach John Vukovich stood on the top dugout step, his eyes riveted on the field. With the practiced stealth of a catburglar Roger snuck up behind Vukovich, and, without drawing any attention to himself, stuck the gum, matches, and *lit cigarette* onto the heel of our coach's Reebok shoe. "Vook" then jogged out to the coach's box to begin the inning.

After Lenny Dykstra strutted into the batter's box, Smith got his sign from catcher Tom Pagnozzi. His first pitch was a fastball over the outer third of the plate, and our gritty leadoff hitter drilled it to left field for a hit. After Dykstra reached first, Vook ordered him to get the signs from third-base coach Larry Bowa.

All the while, the cigarette burned—ever so slowly.

Mickey Morandini was the next batter. After working the count to three balls and a strike, our little second baseman with the short stroke lined Smith's next pitch to right field for another hit. Runners were now on the corners and our best hitter, John Kruk, strolled up to the plate. Vook stood calmly in his coach's box with his hands on his hips and a wad of tobacco in his mouth. The near sellout crowd whipped itself into a frenzy, confident that our most prolific slugger would keep the rally alive.

That's when the trouble started.

Suddenly, a ball of fire erupted from the heel of Vook's shoe. The muscles in his neck tightened, and his eyes grew to the size of grapefruits as he hopped around the Astroturf stomping his foot. "Help, somebody get me some water," he yelled.

But his cry fell on deaf ears. Instead of finding support, he saw only players rolling around laughing at the top of their lungs.

After fanning out the fire, the steaming Vukovich scanned the dugout looking for the guilty party. After a short search his eyes locked onto Roger sitting smugly in the corner. "I know it was you, McDowell. I'm gonna kick your butt." But poor Vukovich could only spend the remainder of the game looking over his shoulder as Roger had retreated to the bullpen to devise his next attack.

McDowell's repertoire included other tricks as he demonstrated it in late June after we completed a series in New York against the Mets. While our bus cruised towards Philadelphia on the New Jersey Turnpike, players made themselves comfortable on the luxury Greyhound by sleeping, flipping through magazines, and playing cards. Roger decided he was not about to sit still for the next two hours. In the rear a high-stakes poker game featured Kruk, Mitch "Wild Thing" Williams, Dave Hollins, and Wally Backman. Cigarette smoke filled the air as the foursome flipped $50 bills around without a care in the world.

Roger strolled towards the action and stood behind Kruk. Unfortunately, over the next three hands, Kruk lost not only $300, but a good deal of patience as well. "Roger, get the hell away from me," snapped the sweet-swinging first baseman.

After slugging down another Budweiser, Backman popped off. "Hey Roger, take a hike."

Hollins dealt the next hand and the trickster slid over behind

131

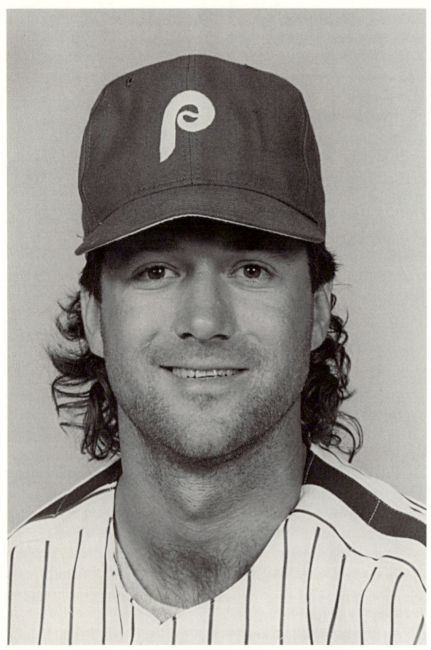

Roger McDowell. (Photo courtesy of the Philadelphia Phillies)

Williams. "Oh no you don't," cried "Wild Thing." "You're not gonna jinx me. Get lost."

But Roger maintained his composure. "OK, guys, if that's what you want, that's fine with me." As Roger turned his back to the group, I watched from a nearby seat with growing interest. I saw Roger reach into his jeans pocket and pull something out. With the game in high gear, Roger nonchalantly dropped what looked like a plastic capsule onto the floor. As soon as it landed he ground it into the floor with the ball of his foot. "OK, you suckers, enjoy the rest of your game," laughed Roger. " I'm outta here."

By the time Roger returned to his seat the time-release capsule had worked to perfection as the smell of rotten eggs created a nauseating, gut-wrenching odor that blanketed the back of the bus. Williams' eyes reddened; Kruk's nostrils flared; Hollins covered his face with a towel; Backman hacked and coughed before firing off a barrage of "f-bombs" so lethal it would have more than earned him a trip to the principal's office and a week's worth of detentions.

Play was halted as the four amigos tried to collect themselves. As Williams leaned forward to pick up a beer bottle, he came upon the broken remains of the powerful stink bomb. As he examined the finger-nail-sized capsule in his hand, he quizzed his playing partners, "Isn't this the spot where Roger was standing?"

Backman popped off again. "I just know Roger was the jerk who planted that stink bomb. I'm gonna kick his butt."

Kruk, a pretty good trickster in his own right, was at the end of his rope with his buddies carping. "Hey Wally, that's some brilliant detective work. Of course it was Roger, you idiot. Now deal the damn cards."

Meanwhile, Roger flipped through a copy of *Field and Stream* magazine without a care in the world. The Phillies' resident prankster had once again gotten the last laugh while most of his teammates gagged their way through the remainder of the trip.

But Roger's hijinks often went beyond fireworks, hotfoots, and stink bombs. Subtlety could be his play also. One afternoon, while stretching

133

in the clubhouse during the seventh inning of a tight game, I noticed that the shoes, shirt, and jeans I'd worn to the park that day had disappeared from my locker. But late-inning maneuvers precluded further investigation.

An hour later, after a heart-breaking loss, I showered and returned to my locker, only to see my clothes back where I had placed them earlier in the day.

But there was one slight problem.

My clothes looked like nothing I had ever seen before. My shirt, jeans, and tennis shoes were all frozen solid, little tufts of frost decorating the sleeves and cuffs. It was as if Mr. Freeze, Batman's icy nemesis, had secretly appeared on the scene, coating my clothes in ice. The arms on my long sleeve denim shirt pointed straight out, making it look like a badly overstarched garment. My jeans were so stiff I would have sworn someone had stuffed half a dozen baseball bats in each leg. My Nike tennis shoes could have been used as giant doorstops.

I foolishly hoped the thawing out process wouldn't take long, so I pulled up a chair and waited. But I quickly realized that unless I was going to drive home wrapped in a white towel, I'd have to consider an alternative wardrobe. So I tore through the bottom of my locker and came up with a red Phillies tee shirt, matching shorts, and the same burgundy turf shoes I'd worn for batting practice that day.

After slipping on my new wardrobe, it didn't take long for my teammates to start giving me the business. Even the notoriously straight-arrowed Dale Murphy had a tough time biting his tongue. "Mo, you gotta be kidding. Is that the best you can do?"

Suddenly, with "Murph" on my case the thought of driving home in my workout clothes got to me. I needed some answers. So I stormed around the clubhouse in a fit of desperation, interrogating my teammates. Still wrapped in naivete, I demanded to know who the mastermind was behind this icy little escapade. And although I never did find out for sure who the guilty party was, all clues pointed to the man I should have suspected all along—Roger McDowell. Heading toward the entrance of the clubhouse I stuck my head inside Roger's locker, searching for any clue that would confirm my suspicion. But the more I gawked at the insides of his cubicle, the more I began to wonder if our ace reliever was part of some secret militia group. A cache of stink bombs, smoke bombs, and firecrackers was piled high on top of his baseball equipment. I realized then that Roger had the capacity to launch a successful attack on any of his teammates at a moment's notice.

Players and coaches were not the only ones subject to Roger's madness. One day while sitting in the dugout, Roger had the attention of one of the batboys. Josh, an enthusiastic nine-year-old, wore a baggy Phillies uniform. An oversized helmet covered the top half of his face. I strolled past the pair and did a doubletake when I heard the faux conspiracy that Roger was luring the boy into.

"Josh, we need your help. We can't start the game until you run up to the clubhouse and get the key to the batter's box."

Poor Josh was eager to help. "I'll be right back," yelled the fleet-footed batboy as he disappeared towards the clubhouse.

Several minutes later Josh returned. His cheeks were flushed and his hands rested on his knees while he tried to catch his breath. "Roger, somebody upstairs told me that the umpires had the key to the batter's box."

Roger had the answer. "Josh, the umpires are standing at homeplate waiting for you. Go on out there and ask them for it."

In a flash, Josh was standing in the middle of the four blue-clad towering giants. They patiently listened to his plea for help, then all four pointed towards the center-field wall. Josh sprinted back towards Roger with the all-important news.

"The umpires say that the key is taped to the flag pole behind the wall in center field. I gotta go!"

Once again, Josh was off to the races.

The game finally began and after a lengthy first inning Josh dragged his body into the dugout. "I couldn't find the key," he puffed. "One of the pitchers in the bullpen told me the key is lost and we should just play the game without it."

For now, Roger's wild goose chase was finished. And so was Josh. Fatigue and exhaustion had wiped him out, and he spent most of the game snuggled in the corner of the dugout, sleeping the sleep of innocence.

For the remainder of the season Roger's pranks, jokes, and escapades continued with regularity. But there were always the moments when he would get down to business to snuff out a late-inning rally with the game on the line. Roger could switch gears and transform himself into the most intense of competitors. The results usually fell in his favor, just as they had for most of his colorful career. But as soon as the game was over, the one thing Roger McDowell's teammates could always count on was that it wouldn't be long before he'd be reaching into his bag of tricks for another way to liven up the day!

"She had a beautiful life of toil and love. All the folks in the entire countryside thought she was wonderful. She has been in my mind all my knowing life and most certainly she is the most unforgettable character I ever knew."
—Branch Rickey

Bottom of the Eighth

MOTHER'S DAY

LIKE MANY LITTLE KIDS, I dreamed of someday becoming a major league baseball player. Unlike other kids, though, I had a mother who encouraged me to make that dream come true. During my junior year of high school, I took pitching lessons from Howie Gershberg, the pitching coach of St. John's University. Baseball scouts started evaluating my arm with great interest. One evening, I came home with the news that St. John's would be interested in giving me a baseball scholarship. Mom greeted the news with a sparkle in her blue eyes and a gorgeous smile on her face. I'd never seen her look more proud and ecstatic. She encouraged me to work hard and take advantage of the opportunity. When more scholarship offers arrived, Mom became my coach, offering advice that ranged from selecting a major to debating the pros and cons of attending an out-of-state college.

In spite of a hectic schedule of raising six children and serving dozens of clients in her dressmaking business, Mom watched me play in many of my high school and collegiate games. After my junior year at Seton Hall, I signed a professional contract and began working my way up in the minor leagues and she flew to such places as Omaha and Louisville just to see me play. Whether or not she was at the game in person, my "number-one fan" was always with me. She always knew how the game had gone. I could fool anyone else, but not Mom. My voice on the telephone gave me away. If it were alive and enthusiastic, she knew I was doing well. If my voice sounded somber or depressed, she figured I was struggling. Usually, she was right.

Ironically, as I moved upward toward my dream of the major leagues, Mom's health began to deteriorate. In the summer of 1986, soon after I was promoted to the major leagues, as an outfielder for the Cardinals, Mom was diagnosed with breast cancer. Over the next few years, she endured three operations, dozens of chemotherapy sessions, and numerous drugs.

I longed to be home on Long Island with Mom to share her ordeal, but the Cardinals' baseball schedule made it difficult. I prayed for a berth with a team closer to New York. Finally, my wish came true. When my five-year career with the Cardinals came to an end after the 1990 season, I signed a contract with the Philadelphia Phillies—just three short hours away from Mom's home.

During the first half of my season with the Phillies, Mom's condition worsened. By the summer of 1991, there was no longer any doubt: My mother was dying. The cancer had invaded her brain, creating problems with balance and coordination. As her condition became more hopeless, my fiancée, Linda, and I decided to move up our November wedding and get married during the All-Star break so that Mom could attend.

Our wedding day—July 9, 1991—was a beautiful day, made all the more beautiful by my mother's joy and humor that remained strong, despite her failing body. She had a wonderful time. The wedding reception was held at J. Paul's Long Island restaurant, owned by my friend Joe Bonin. Threading her way between tables, Mom greeted and joked with as many of our 40 guests as she could. She seemed to have a special gracious word for each person. I had to fight my way through the crowd to reach her side.

Our wedding day. Surrounded by Linda and Grace.

"Mom," I said, somewhat breathless, "let's dance."

"I thought you'd never ask," she replied.

The song was "Unchained Melody," the theme from the movie *Ghost*. As we danced slowly in the middle of the crowded floor, I felt her small body sink in my arms. It seemed that I might break her if I squeezed too hard. But I sensed that she wanted to be held, so I comforted her as best as I could. Not a word passed between us. When the

139

song finished, we just looked at each other. We were both conscious of a feeling of love that words can't describe.

After the All-Star break, my performance as a player, which was such a source of joy and pride, began to slide. Phillies manager, Jim Fregosi, inserted Lenny Dykstra, back off the disabled list, in the regular lineup. As a result, I began accumulating some serious bench time. My batting average began to drop. Over the course of the next six weeks, I proceeded to go hitless in 18 consecutive at-bats. For an everyday player, that kind of slump usually takes only about four or five days, but for a utility bench player, that time can seem like an eternity.

I called Mom every day, but avoided talking about my batting slump. In fact, she was feeling so ill that we rarely even discussed baseball. I began to feel helpless. My poor performance and my concern for Mom began to affect my whole life. I didn't want people to feel sorry for me so rather than tell my teammates about my problems, I kept them to myself. I often found myself sitting in a far corner of the dugout, avoiding my teammates. Good-natured teasing began to hurt tremendously. I never felt so alone. Even Linda became the target of my silent frustration. I internalized everything. Linda would ask, "What's wrong? Are you all right?" I would growl, "Nothing! I'm fine!" My strong silent number was building a wall that not even my beautiful wife could get through.

Denis Menke, the Phillies' hitting instructor, eventually got me out of my rut and headed in the right direction. I'd worked with Denis all during the season. He was a cheerful Irishman, a man I respected. Denis was always fair, treating all the players the same, and shrugged off taking credit for himself. I had come to trust him completely. Denis understood about Mom's illness and what I was going through. He never passed me without a hand on my shoulder or a quiet, "Hang in there, Johnny."

Finally, Denis was the one who took on breaking down my wall. He walked up to me in the dugout, looked me firmly in the eye, and announced, "It's time we had a talk. I have something that might help your hitting."

That day, I wasn't up for a conversation, much less a batting lesson. But when Denis had that edge in his voice, I knew he meant business. He had me try something entirely new, lowering my hand to the middle of my chest and holding the bat vertically.

"Johnny, I want you to think of meeting the ball out in front," he said. "The ball has been getting too deep on you, and that's why you've been making lousy contact."

With Denis Menke throwing batting practice, I spent the next 30 minutes successfully hitting balls in the indoor batting cage at Veterans Stadium. My new approach felt great. My swing was now shorter and quicker, giving me a better chance to drive the ball with authority. The idea of meeting the ball in front of the plate reminded me that I needed to be quick and aggressive. Concentrating on improving my batting average was lifting me out of my fog of depression.

"Denis, this feels great," I said. "Let's hope I can take it into the game."

"Johnny," he said with a grin, "there's nothing wrong with your swing. The next time you hit, just make sure you get a good pitch to hit. And be *aggressive.*"

Several days after my lesson with Menke, my batting slump ended explosively. It was September 1, 1991, a gorgeous Sunday afternoon in Philadelphia where we were hosting the Atlanta Braves. The score was tied , 4-4, when I entered the game as a leadoff pinch hitter in the bottom of the 10th inning. I was sent in to hit against one of the hardest throwing right-handed pitchers in the league at the time, Mark Wohlers. My determination was to do *anything* just to get on base. For Mom. For Linda. For myself. I began to feel as if I was stepping back into my life.

I looked at the first two pitches, allowing the count to reach a ball and a strike. Swinging at the next two fastballs, both clocked in excess of 95 MPH, I managed to foul both off and stay alive. It was after those two healthy cuts that I felt something that had been missing for a long time—a renewed sense of my competitive spirit. Somehow, for no reason I could put my finger on, I knew this time at-bat would be different. Suddenly, I could put it all aside—the pain, the confusion, the doubts, and focus on the game that had been my life since I was a child.

I took the next pitch for ball two, high and away, then followed with late swings to produce two weak foul balls down the left-field line. With the count now at two balls and two strikes, I stepped out of the batter's box, mentally preparing for the hardest pitch my adversary could possibly throw. Remembering Menke's advice about meeting the ball in front of the plate, I was determined to not swing late again.

Back in the batter's box, I waited for the right pitch. Wohlers went through his windup and released a fastball towards the inside corner of the plate. I felt a total freedom as I began my swing.

Crack! The ball exploded off my bat. It was the type of thunderous crack usually created by superstar sluggers. As I ran for first base, I watched right fielder David Justice running full-tilt for the outfield wall. He made a tremendous leap—scrambling up the wall with his arm fully extended—but the ball sailed high over the fence for the game-winning home run. Trotting around the bases, I felt my heart pumping so fast it seemed about to burst through my uniform jersey. At homeplate I was mobbed by my teammates. The feeling of elation was so wonderful that I wished it could last forever. The only thing missing was that Mom wasn't there.

After the game, "Video Dan," our video production manager, handed me a videotape.

"You might want to take a look at this, Johnny," he said. "It's something you'll want to keep for a long time."

Several days after my home run, I visited Mom. My sister Karen, who had taken a leave of absence from her job to care of Mom, was attending to her needs when I arrived. The illness was progressing at an alarming rate. Chronic fatigue sapped Mom's energy and she spent most of the day in bed. Unable to go up or down stairs, she was restricted to her bedroom and an adjacent upstairs den. With a pang of sorrow, I sensed that this would probably be the last real visit we would have.

Spring training, 1991, in Clearwater, FL. (Photo courtesy of The Philadelphia Phillies)

143

Helping her to her feet, I escorted her to the den. She seemed weightless. My once vivacious mother had shrunken to less than 90 pounds. Even the simple act of getting out of bed exhausted her. Her bones creaked with every step she took.

The den was a small sunny room with a large-screen TV and a VCR. I sat her in a comfortable chair directly in front of the television, close enough for her to see with her failing eyesight. Although one of her eyes was covered with a bandage, Mom insisted that she could see the TV just fine. I inserted the tape in the VCR and pressed play. Since I hadn't viewed the tape, I was as interested as Mom to see what would unfold. Mom and I held hands as we watched and listened.

Veteran announcer, Harry Kalas, was doing the play-by-play. After I hit the game-winning home run, he said, "John Morris has really struggled this second half of the season, and this couldn't have happened to a nicer guy."

A lump appeared in my throat and tears welled in my eyes as Kalas showed a slow-motion replay of the dramatic home run. As Wohlers went into his windup, Kalas in his strong, polished delivery, added, "John's mother has been quite ill for some time." He paused for a second as if empathizing with my long ordeal. That one-second delay allowed the ball and bat to connect, thus allowing one of the game's finest announcers to finish his thought: "And this one was probably for his mom."

Mom and I looked at each other, our eyes brimming, our cheeks wet. It was an incredibly intimate moment. Mom hugged me as tightly as she was able and whispered, "I love you, son, and I'm very proud of you. I'm going to miss you very much."

On the last weekend of September, just as the season was ending, I received a phone call from my brother, Stephen.

"Johnny," he said, "you better get up here. Mom isn't expected to last through the weekend."

I drove from Philadelphia to her Long Island home as quickly as possible. I was shocked by her condition. Cancer had ravaged her to the point where she was nearly unrecognizable. Her body was skeletal; veins appeared ready to rip through skin and bony arms. Her once beautiful face was blurred, and I knew she could no longer see me. Her breathing was labored. Even the breathing machine struggled to help.

Tears filled my eyes and I had to leave the room. In the den where we had watched the videotape, I sat and wept. Stephen sat with me. Linda remained behind with Mom, holding her hand and stroking her. Linda inserted Mom's favorite CD into the stereo. When I reentered the room, they were listening to George Winston's *December*.

The last out of the 1991 baseball season was recorded Sunday afternoon, October 6th. Early Monday morning, October 7th, Grace Theresa Morris passed on as I sat alone with her at her bedside. It was almost as if she knew the season was complete, and that it was indeed okay for her to let go.

145

"Luck is a fact, but should not be a factor. Good luck is what is leftover after intelligence and effort have combined at their best. Negligence or indifference or inattention are usually reviewed from an unlucky seat. Luck is the residue of design."

—Branch Rickey

Top of the Ninth

ANGEL ON THE JERSEY TURNPIKE

MONTHS AFTER MY SEASON with the Phillies ended, I signed a free-agent contract with the California Angels. During my first spring training in the Cactus League, I batted over .400 and earned a spot on the Halos' opening-day roster. The thought of playing in the American League against perennial contenders like the Yankees, Red Sox, and Royals made my body tingle with excitement. I didn't have to wait very long for my wish to come true.

It was May 20, 1992. We had just finished the sixth game of a nine-game road trip taking us through Boston, New York, and Baltimore. Our team looked both physically and mentally exhausted as the dog days of summer approached.

The last out of the third game with the New York Yankees had been recorded at 10:25 P.M. The "Bronx Bombers" had pummeled us for three straight losses in the series. As soon as we were done showering and picking over the post-game spread, it was off to Baltimore to play the Orioles.

I climbed aboard the second of the two buses and settled in for the three-hour ride. A short time later, we were on the road, racing through the Bronx. Our drivers took corners like Indy car drivers. I imagined that they knew the dangers of driving through the South Bronx at night, and I applauded their sense of urgency. It seemed as if only minutes had passed before we found ourselves at the southbound entrance to the New Jersey Turnpike. Next stop, Baltimore—or so I thought.

For the first hour I fidgeted in my seat watching the scenery fly past my window. Other players watched a movie on the overhead TV monitors, or listened to personal stereos. A few slept. In the rear of the bus, a half dozen of our pitchers were involved in a high-stakes poker game. A sign for Exit 4, Philadelphia/Camden, caught my eye and I knew we were making great time.

Suddenly, our bus driver slammed on the breaks and swerved to the right. Players caught off guard were tossed around the cabin like rag dolls. The bus slid to a screeching halt on the shoulder of the road. Still in shock, we picked ourselves up and tried to figure out what had happened.

Several voices began yelling at once. "Bus one is down, bus one is down." Through the windows I could see a cloud of dust, debris, and broken tree limbs. The highway guardrail had been torn to shreds.

As the dust settled, I could make out the shape of the lead bus some 50 yards away. It lay on its side, the front end crushed like a tin can and dangling precariously over a running stream some 10 feet below. Three oak trees held it in place and kept it from falling into the murky waters.

I scrambled off our bus with the rest of the players and heard loud screams from teammates inside the wreck. Because of its precarious position, any attempt to board the downed bus might have sent it tumbling into the stream. A heavy smell of fuel added to our feelings of panic and helplessness.

That's when I saw him—our pitcher, Chuck Finley—inside the wreck helping his teammates. I'd last seen Chuck in the card game in the back of our bus, his sleeves rolled up, deeply engaged in a serious

Chuck Finley. (Photo courtesy of the National Baseball Hall of Fame Library, Cooperstown, NY)

game of five-card draw. Somehow, he'd managed to get past us and board the wreck. Nobody had the foggiest idea how he'd done it.

Born and raised in Monroe, Louisiana, Chuck Finley stood a mighty 6'6" and weighed a healthy 215 pounds. Looking like a rock star, he had long brown hair, a narrow face, dark eyes, and strong cheekbones standing above the two-day growth of beard he favored. True to his appearance, he could often be heard cranking out favorite tunes from Led Zeppelin and The Moody Blues on his Fender electric guitar in an empty room near the home clubhouse.

Chuck was a veteran left-handed pitcher of eight seasons with the Angels. He had a lively fastball that routinely clocked around 90 MPH, and an overhand curveball that dropped straight down. Chuck was a first-class competitor—exactly the type of pitcher you wanted on the mound when the game was on the line.

Now he was on a wrecked bus, placing himself in danger to help his teammates. We stood around looking stunned and not knowing exactly what to do as Chuck performed his superman imitation, kicking out windows and pulling teammates from beneath mangled seats. His lead got us moving in the right direction, helping him as he lowered injured players through the openings. Even uninjured teammates on the wrecked bus began to assist.

Within minutes, everyone was off the wreck and receiving assistance—or so we thought. But a hasty head count showed that Buck Rodgers, our manager who had been seated in the front row, was nowhere to be found. Checking through the wreck, catcher Mike Fitzgerald spotted a body trapped under the seat directly behind the driver's seat. It was Buck.

It took several players to clear enough wreckage to get Buck off the bus. The time it took felt like hours. Once out of the wreck, we put him down gently on the damp grass. His hair was covered with blood, his eyes were closed, and his body felt limp and lifeless. If he wasn't dead, he was certainly critically injured. Suddenly, Buck moved his leg. Bert Blyleven, a veteran pitcher of 20-plus seasons, knelt next to him and said, "Buck, you're gonna to be fine."

Buck let out a brief moan, then said, "Of course, I'm gonna be fine, as soon as you get off my leg you idiot."

Buck was alive, and so was his sense of humor.

Injured players included second baseman Bobby Rose who required 50 stitches to close an ugly head wound, and Alvan Davis whose bruised kidneys caused him to discharge blood for over a week. Several other players suffered from broken ribs, stiff necks, and various degrees of whiplash. Fortunately, there were no fatalities.

We were stranded on the turnpike for the next hour. Eventually, we were transported to a truck stop by another bus and allowed to telephone our families. It was an emotional time for us, knowing how close we came to losing teammates. Some players cried openly while others had dazed looks on their faces.

The news didn't get any better the next day. Players Rose and Davis were placed on the disabled list and Buck Rodgers was lost for the remainder of the season, allowing John Wathan, our third-base coach, to take over the managerial reigns. Buck's injuries were the most serious- a shattered elbow and a blown-out knee both requiring surgery, and broken ribs which made his breathing difficult and painful.

The accident caused our already low team spirit to hit rock bottom. There was no rallying cry to perform for our fallen skipper. Instead, we glumly played out the schedule, waiting for the season to end so we could go home and forget it'd ever happened.

Two weeks later, I finally had a chance to talk to Chuck Finley about the incident. We had just completed another unsuccessful road trip and Chuck was giving me a ride home from the airport. "So, Chuck," I began, "how'd you manage to get on bus #1 so fast when everybody knew you were playing cards in the back of bus #2?"

A smile appeared on Chuck's face as he began to speak. "When I was a kid growing up in Louisiana, my dad used to drive me up and down the country roads looking for accident victims and broken down cars. Many times we'd pull cars out of ditches or help people out who were injured. Dad taught me early on in life that helping people out was the right thing to do."

I was impressed. I felt like I was sitting next to the Cajun Caped Crusader from the Bayou. But it wasn't until I'd said good-bye that I realized that Chuck had done a masterful job of avoiding my question. I never did find out how Chuck got to that wreck so fast. But I can take a hint. Chuck is not interested in taking credit or considering himself as a hero.

Over the last dozen years, Chuck Finley has been one of the most impressive left-handed pitchers in baseball. He has more career wins than any pitcher in Angels history and has been named to the All-Star team several times. But those accomplishments pale in comparison to his heroic efforts in the Angels' bus crash of 1992. On that night, Chuck distinguished himself as a compassionate and caring human being—the kind of person who grew up practicing random acts of kindness and never stopped.

"Baseball is a fun game. When the game began to be a job, that bothered me. That's why I quit, when it began to be work. In baseball, at a certain age, you have to get out. You can't go back. There is nothing to go back to."
—Willie Mays

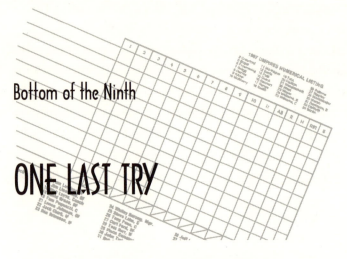

Bottom of the Ninth

ONE LAST TRY

JUDGING FROM THE EXPRESSIONS I'd seen over the previous years, few things were sadder in baseball than the face of a teammate as he received the news that "his baseball services are no longer required." It didn't matter if it was 20-year-old stuck in Class-A ball or a veteran major leaguer holding on for one more big payday. The ritual of a player's release usually signaled the end of a boyhood dream.

In August of 1992, after years avoiding the inevitable, I found my own head on baseball's chopping block. Our team, the California Angels, floundered in the basement of the American League Western Division. My batting average hovered around the .200 mark, two players were set to come off the disabled list, and outfielder Tim Salmon was destroying Triple-A pitching and certain to be promoted. I suspected that a few heads were about to roll.

So when coach Ken Macha approached me and whispered, "Dan O'Brien [the general manager] wants to see you," I couldn't say I was surprised. Even though I'd prepared myself for this possibility, I was still scared to death. My knees shook as I headed into the manager's office.

Minutes later, I walked out as an unemployed 31-year-old baseball player looking for a job. I returned home to Florida, hoping that any team would call for the stretch drive.

But the phone didn't ring.

Finally, later that winter, the Pittsburgh Pirates called and invited me to the 1993 major league camp. General manager Ted Simmons assured me that I'd get every chance to make the big league team.

My baseball spirit was rekindled, knowing I'd be playing for Pirates skipper Jim Leyland. As manager of the Bucs since 1986, Leyland's teams had improved each season before they won three consecutive Eastern Division championships from 1990 to 1992. Leyland was a proven winner. He was the type of manager I'd love to play for.

Spring training was finally upon us and I reported to the Pirates' spring training facility in Bradenton, Florida. The morning of the first workout I felt a tap on my shoulder. It was Leyland. "John," he started, "we're happy to have you on board. If you need anything, let me know." I began to tell him how excited I was to be in camp. He sucked on a Marlboro as his eyes shifted around the room. Thirty seconds later, our intro ended as Leyland darted across the room to greet a handful of other players.

My first days in camp went well. I was relaxed, confident, and motivated. Finally, after a week of batting practice, drills, and conditioning, it was time to play ball as the exhibition season began. But my optimism quickly turned to concern after I pulled a hamstring legging out an infield hit in my first at-bat. For a week, I was unable to do more than fill the whirlpool every day so I could float around in the vessel my teammates aptly named the *USS Morris*. After eventually receiving clearance from the trainers to play, I figured Leyland would throw me into some games as soon as possible. But in my first two games back, I was relegated to the bench. Not being given a chance to play seemed strange because I was healthy. Maybe Leyland wanted to give me an extra day or two to recover from my injury. Secretly, I hoped he knew what he was doing.

On my third day back our team traveled to St. Petersburg to play the Baltimore Orioles. I was hopeful I'd be in the starting lineup. But once again I was disappointed, left to wonder when my next chance would come.

Following batting practice, I shagged balls in right field. After completing my work I saw Leyland heading in my direction. A fungo bat twirled in his fingers and his head hung as he moved towards me. I suspected he was coming over to offer some words of encouragement. Closing the distance between us to three feet, he stood to my left as we faced the infield together. Once again his eyes shifted away. He began to speak in a reserved tone.

"John, we're going to send you to the minor league camp," he said. "You'll start the season in Buffalo [Triple-A]. I'm not gonna make any promises. If someone gets hurt, I'm gonna call up the guy who's the hottest."

I shook my head several times to make sure I wasn't in the midst of a terrible dream.

Leyland fidgeted in his stance as he continued, "Sorry things didn't work out for you. Just go down to Buffalo, work hard, and we'll see what happens during the season."

In the blink of an eye he was gone. I fumed in stony silence as Leyland stalked across the outfield towards another soon-to-be dejected player.

The start of the game sent me to a spot in the dugout. "I don't deserve this, I'm getting screwed," kept echoing in my head. All I wanted was to get in my car, drive the three miles to my home, and hide from the rest of the world. I was furious and couldn't have cared less if I ever saw Jim Leyland or the Pittsburgh Pirates again. But instead, I sulked on the bench as nine long, ghost-like innings played themselves out on the field.

As soon as the game ended, I tore off my uniform, dressed, and trudged outside. Linda was waiting for me in the parking lot. One look at me and she knew something wasn't right. "What's the matter?" she asked. Before I could say a word, tears filled my eyes. "It's back to Triple-A, Linda. But tomorrow morning I'm gonna ask for my release." I wasn't finished. "Can you believe they shipped me out after giving me one at-bat? What a bunch of crap."

Linda spent the rest of the evening enduring my whining and complaining.

The following morning I was at the Pirates' minor league complex to see farm director Chet Montgomery. Steam was still coming from my ears as I entered his office.

"Chet," I began, cutting right to the chase, "I'd like to have my release."

He appeared a bit surprised by my request. "Your contract states that if you didn't make the big club, you'd go to Triple-A." Chet paused briefly, leaned forward in his chair and rested his chin on his hands. "But given the fact you played in only one game, I can see why you're so pissed off. I'd never want to keep you from getting back to the big leagues, John. And it's obvious you'd rather be somewhere else. So I'm gonna give you your release."

My wish had been granted. But I now had no idea what future I had left in pro ball. Would another team want me? Or had I just signed my own death certificate by asking for my release? I was still confident I could perform at the major league level, but I figured my best chance to get there would have to come with another organization. After all, if Leyland had had me in his plans for the upcoming season, I would have gotten more playing time during camp. But with the spring training clock ticking, I also realized that my options were limited.

The drive home over the Sunshine Skyway Bridge gave me plenty of time to think. As I took the exit ramp off Interstate 275, I detoured to Al Lang Stadium where the Cardinals were playing that afternoon. As the team practiced on the field I strolled around the clubhouse and chatted with trainers and clubhouse personnel.

In a stroke of luck, I bumped into Cardinals farm director Mike Jorgensen. Years earlier, Mike had been my manager when I played in

Louisville. After a long career in the majors, he now was overseeing the Cards' minor league system. Mike's face lit up as he extended his hand. "Hey, Morris," he said. "Nice to see you. I thought you were with the Pirates."

"Mike," I sighed, "I just got my release this morning. Things didn't work out."

Jorgensen's eyes widened. "Well, how would you like to play center field every day for us in Triple-A? We need an outfielder and this could be a great opportunity for you."

My interest was piqued, but I was curious. "Mike, give me a day to think about it. I'll call you back."

That evening, Linda played the role of coach and offered a variety of perspectives. "If you go to Triple-A, you can find out a few things," she started. "You'll get to play every day for the first time in seven years. That's great! And you'll get to see how much your body can withstand. But the best part is you'll have a chance to get back to St. Louis. You always told me your most enjoyable years in baseball were with the Cardinals."

Linda made sense. Suddenly, the thought of playing Triple-A had a certain appeal to it.

I called Mike the next day and accepted his offer, and, within a few days, I was sharing a clubhouse with 150 other minor leaguers. I was now 32 years old—no longer the young rising star I was a decade earlier. Twenty-year-old rookies began asking me for advice. Many of them wanted to know about the good old days when the Cardinals of the 1980s terrorized the National League with their blazing speed. Being around so many young faces made me think about my own career, and how quickly it had gone.

With spring training winding down, extra batting practice and wind sprints were on the daily agenda, and by opening day I was ready for the upcoming 140-game schedule.

The season began in early April with a week-long homestand against the Oklahoma City 89ers and the Iowa Cubs. I got off to a hot start, stroking nine hits in my first 25 five at-bats as we pounded both teams into submission. I was playing every day for the first time in years, and having the time of my life.

But red flags suddenly went up at the tail end of the homestand. My back had flared up again, and an old groin injury kept me from running at full speed. Over the next 12 days, we traveled to New Orleans, Iowa, and Omaha. By the time we arrived in Omaha for the final series of the road trip, the frigid midwestern temperatures made it virtually impossible to get loose. My batting stroke had also stiffened and I collected just one hit in 12 at-bats. But as sore and stiff as I felt, I was determined to be ready for the next game.

Playing on natural grass for 12 consecutive days provided some much-needed relief for my body, but now we headed back to the wornout Astroturf in Louisville for 10 games. By the time the third game was over, the simple act of bending over to tie my shoelaces hurt like hell. The season was barely a month old and I was begging not only for rainouts but also for the whole damn season to end.

A week later we were on the road to Oklahoma City. Prior to the opener, rain drenched the field, causing a two-hour delay. As the game unfolded, I sloshed about in a drizzle, and the simple task of jogging on and off the field through mud and wet grass became increasingly difficult. By the time the marathon ended, my back hurt so badly I could barely stand up.

The following day I was at the park hours early so trainer Brad Bluestone could go to work on me. "I know you're hurting," said Brad. "If you need a day off, let me know."

I appreciated Brad's offer, but I figured I could play if I took the time to stretch my legs and do my back exercises. For nine long innings I struggled on both offense and defense. In four at-bats, I tapped back to the pitcher twice and rolled two grounders to the second baseman. On defense I had trouble getting to balls that would have been a routine out weeks earlier.

After the game, the strained expression on my face was all Brad needed to see. "Johnny, we're gonna shut you down for a few days."

"No complaints here," I mumbled. "I don't know how much more my body can take anyway."

Brad and I, along with manager Jack Krol, came up with a plan that we hoped would provide some relief. "We're going to give you the next four games off," offered Krol, "and then we'll take it from there."

Four days later Jack approached me, "How ya doing?"

"I'm ready. Let's go," I fired back.

The Nashville Sounds, the Triple-A affiliate of the Chicago White Sox, were in town. I was back in the starting lineup and ready to face a tough righty named Jason Bere. A wicked slider and forkball complemented the young phenom's nasty fastball.

In the first inning I came to the plate with the bases loaded and two out. I took Bere's first offering for strike one. I swung at the next pitch—a room-service fastball right down the middle of the plate but flared a jam shot into the third-base stands as my bat splintered into several pieces. Seconds later, I returned to the batter's box with a new Louisville Slugger and a hint of embarrassment on my face. Bere was poised to finish me off. He unleashed a vicious forkball. I flailed away, missing the ball as it short hopped into the catcher's mitt.

From that point on, the game only got worse. I finished the contest 0-for-4 with three punchouts and a popout to the catcher.

The following morning I awoke unable to move. Lying in bed, my body throbbed and just breathing made my back hurt.

Linda helped roll me onto my side. I finally made my way out of bed onto the floor where I lay motionless for several minutes. "Linda," I said, "this is ridiculous. It's time to call it a career."

"Johnny," she said, "I don't want to see you get hurt anymore. And it would be nice if you were able to walk after you were done playing."

I called Krol and asked to meet with him when I got to the park that afternoon. Hours later, I hobbled into the clubhouse. Krol was already in his office.

"Jack,'" I sighed, "it's time to call it quits before I totally blow my back out again."

Jack Krol. (Photo courtesy of the National Baseball Hall of Fame Library, Cooperstown, NY)

Jack responded, "Hey, I know you've been struggling. I can see the pain in your eyes. But I also want you to be 100-percent sure of your decision."

Then he added, "I have a favor to ask. I'd like you to hang around for a couple of days and just watch the games. You don't even have to get dressed. If, after two games you don't miss playing, then you should retire. But if you feel the urge to be out there, I'd love to have you stay for the rest of the season."

I locked my hands behind my head and considered his proposal. "I appreciate the offer. I'll hang around for a few days, but I don't really think it's gonna make a difference."

That evening I sat quietly on the bench and watched our team cruise to an easy win. I had no burning desire to be part of the action, probably because the mere thought of playing made my bones rattle.

The following day was a beautiful day for baseball. The sun shone brightly, and the temperature was in the mid-70s. A slight breeze blew across the stands. If I were ever going to miss being on the ballfield, this would be the day.

I decided to watch the game from the bullpen behind the left-field fence. I studied our new center fielder—budding superstar Brian Jordan—and I tried unsuccessfully to envision myself in the game. Over the next three hours, I watched Jordan roam the outfield with a splendid combination of power, speed, and grace. He had all the makings of a quality major leaguer. Watching him reminded me that professional baseball is a game for the young and strong, for those capable of withstanding the daily grind.

During breaks in the action my eyes drifted around the stadium. I noted the efforts of the five-man grounds crew as they scrambled between the bases in the middle of the fifth inning with rakes and replacement bags in hand. I watched vendors weave their way through the grandstands, hawking everything from hot dogs to yearbooks and wondered how many hundreds of players they'd seen play in Redbird Stadium over the decades. My eyes shot up at the radio box and I

Brian Jordan. (Photo courtesy of the National Baseball Hall of Fame Library, Cooperstown, NY)

wondered if Ed Peek, the long time voice of the Redbirds, would ever get a taste of the big leagues. During the seventh inning stretch, "Take Me Out to the Ball Game" never sounded so good as 7,000 booming voices cranked out baseball's favorite song. It sent chills down my spine. Little kids stood behind the outfield fence and pounded their gloves, waiting for a slugger to send a homer in their direction so they could go home with a lucky souvenir.

In the bottom of the eighth inning Jordan was back on center stage. He laced a hanging breaking ball to the right-center field gap and smelled extra bases as he bolted from the batter's box. His legs churned

"Even if I never get one more big-league at bat, I'm a lucky person. I lived my dream."—J.M., Louisville Redbirds, April 1993 (Photo by Larry Spitzer and courtesy of The Courier-Journal*)*

coming around second base as he headed for third. The relay throw to the third baseman was right on the money, but Jordan's textbook hook slide avoided the tag. "Way to go, Brian," I yelled. "Now *that's* the way to play the game."

After the game I hobbled into Jack's office. We looked at each other before I spoke. "Hey, great game today, Jack. But to be honest with you, nothing has changed. Thanks for asking me to hang around for a few extra days. It gave me the chance to be sure of my decision."

We shook hands and I left his office for the last time. I said my good-byes and wished my teammates well. Though some appeared indifferent, others appeared saddened by my departure.

Stepping into retirement no longer seemed like such an awful thought. Being able to do it on my own terms, with the organization that provided my fondest memories was the greatest gift I could have given myself. On May 15, 1993, on a picture perfect day in Louisville, Kentucky, I walked out of the clubhouse for the last time as a player.

It was time to get on with the rest of my life.

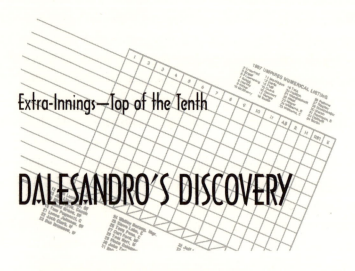

Extra-Innings—Top of the Tenth

DALESANDRO'S DISCOVERY

MARK DALESANDRO MADE the California Angels major league team coming out of the 1995 spring training. A tough Italian kid who grew up on the southside of Chicago, he attended the University of Illinois on a baseball scholarship in the early 1990s. At his best on third base, Mark was a valuable utility player who could man several different positions. But his greatest assets were his offensive capabilities and aggressive style of play. A line-drive hitter with a compact swing, Mark played baseball with the kind of enthusiasm and passion that Pete Rose would have admired.

Mark stood only 5'10" and weighed 190 pounds. He possessed rugged good looks with brown eyes, jet-black hair that was feathered straight back, and an olive tone to a healthy complexion. His frame was well defined but not enormous. His arms were a display of finely toned biceps, triceps, and Popeye-sized forearms.

Unfortunately, for a variety of reasons, Mark's major league season in 1995 didn't last very long. In mid-May, after only a handful of plate appearances, Mark was optioned to the minors.

I was the batting coach for the California Angels' Triple-A team in Vancouver, British Columbia. The year before, I made my coaching debut when the Angels hired me to coach their Double-A Team in Midland, Texas. Now, after a season in the Permian Basin, just several hours from the west Texas town of El Paso, I'd earned a promotion to the scenic Pacific Northwest. During that season, I had the pleasure of working with many fine players. Highlights of the season included our team making the playoffs and sending 20 players to the major leagues during the season. But as rewarding as the season was for all involved, there was one experience that made this particular campaign very special for me.

Mark joined our team and quickly became a valuable player, able to play first base, third base, and the outfield. He even proved to be a capable catcher when needed. He didn't care what position he played as long as his name was on the lineup card. With constant playing time, his batting average hovered at the .330 in his first two months.

However, things changed quickly following the All-Star break in mid-July. For the first time in his pro career, Mark went into a prolonged batting slump. He began struggling with all facets of his game. But the thing that frustrated him most was his hitting. The slump began on an eight-game road trip through Calgary and Edmonton and continued into a 12-game homestand. In that three-week period Mark's batting average dropped to .260, the lowest it had been all season.

As batting coach, it was my job to get him going again. I was confident that Mark would eventually come out of his funk. I began putting in extra time with him and we tried several approaches to get him back on track. We adjusted his hand position hoping it would shorten his swing. We focused on having Mark drive the ball through the middle of the field so he would avoid pulling off the ball. We were willing to try anything. But part of the problem was that Mark never stuck with anything long enough to see if it worked. If he had a few bad games, it was time to try something else.

Mark was edgy about his lack of performance and I soon began to feel a sense of urgency working with him. I also became aware of his

Mark Dalesandro. (Photo courtesy of the National Baseball Hall of Fame Library, Cooperstown, NY)

lack of confidence, and how much distance he placed between himself and his teammates. But the good thing about Mark was that he could be counted on to keep trying. Like the main character in the *Rocky* movies, he would keep fighting and scrapping.

Mark continued to be frustrated into early August when our team traveled to Salt Lake City to begin a series against the Buzz, the Triple-A team of the Minnesota Twins. Badly outmatched in all facets of the game, we lost the first three. Mark's abysmal play continued as he managed just one hit in 12 plate appearances. It was his lone hit in his last 40 at-bats and his average was down to .230. After the third game, I remember how depressed he looked as he sat at his locker, his back to the room in an attempt to isolate himself from his teammates. He slumped in a chair and stared aimlessly at the ceiling.

The following day, Mark played left field. His misery continued as he went hitless in five plate appearances, producing three strikeouts and two weak rollers to the shortstop. After his final out, Mark angrily hurled bats, gloves, and anything else he could get his hands on while cursing himself out unmercifully. His batting average was approaching the .220 mark and the prospects of a quick turnaround did not appear likely.

The mood in clubhouse after the game was somber. I was picking at a piece of rubber chicken from the post-game spread when our trainer Don McGann approached me. "Hey, Mo, Dalesandro's down in the batting cage. You might wanna go check on him."

The game had been over for 20 minutes. I nervously worked my way down the long narrow corridor to the batting cages, unsure of what awaited me. As I opened the door, Mark crushed a ball off a batting tee into the far end of the cage. "That sucks!" he screamed. I watched as Mark beat another dozen balls off the tee at a furious pace. Sweat poured off his face as each swing produced more self-analysis and four-letter expletives.

I took a seat outside the cage area and watched him unleash 10 more vicious hacks. Grunts, groans, and vulgarity continued to fill the air. I finally spoke up. "Hey, Mark," I called, "how many more balls you gonna hit?"

Mark's breathing was labored and his words came fast. "Hey, Mo, I ain't leaving here till you help me fix what's wrong. I don't care if it takes all night. I'm stayin' till I get my act together." I rolled my eyes at the thought of spending several more hours caged up in this dusty sweatbox with a madman. We were looking at a very long evening.

Mark finally ran out of balls. He had turned the inside of the batting cage into his personal driving range. Dozens of white balls blanketed the green turf as the two of us went to work picking them up. All Mark wanted was to get the balls back in the bucket so he could begin his assault again. I knew I had to do something drastic.

"Hey, Mark," I started, "I see exactly what's wrong with your swing. Give me your bat and I'll show you what the problem is." Mark was more than happy to hand me his C271 Louisville Slugger. Mark stared at me hopefully as I cradled his bat in my fingers. But I had no plans, no ideas. So I did the first thing that came into my head. I wound up and threw his bat as hard as I could to the other end of the cage. Mark and I watched as the bat lazily tumbled through the air some 90 feet, bouncing off the far end of the cage and rolling to a stop on the turf.

Mark turned to me, a puzzled look on his face. "What the hell are you doing? I thought you were gonna help me?"

I pointed towards the ground and groaned, "Sit down, we need to talk." Suddenly, I was struck with a feeling of déjà vu. All I could see was myself years earlier as a struggling Triple-A veteran in Omaha and Louisville. I held an image of managers Gene Lamont and Jim Fregosi, and I grinned at the thought of the mental gymnastics they often used to set me straight. Whether it was a subtle pat on the back or a verbal tongue lashing, I felt secure knowing someone was on my side. Now, a decade later I would try my hand at helping another Triple-A vet escape from his minor league hell hole.

The tension inside the cage was thick. I knew Mark was in no mood for a talk, but at least I had his undivided attention.

For the first minute or so, our conversation centered on his poor baseball performance. But I quickly ran out of physical and mechanical suggestions. It was time for a new strategy. Taking a gamble, I steered the conversation away from baseball. "Mark, is there anything off the field that's bothering you?"

Mark hesitated for a second, but the door was open. "Well," he began, "I've got a lot of crap going on with my fiancée right now. We've been arguing a lot lately."

There was no stopping him now. The issues were numerous and complex. I sat and listened until he ran down.

"Anything else?" I asked.

Again he paused before launching into a series of issues concerning his parents. "I'm not on good speaking terms with my dad," he began. "He's been on my case pretty hard lately. Every time I talk to him on the phone he wants to know why I'm not in the big leagues." Mark went on to tell me about his best friend who had been killed in an auto accident, and another who had legal problems and was spending time in jail.

When he was finished, I asked, "Anything else you wanna say?" Mark scratched at the black stubble on his chin, then took a deep breath. "Ya know, Mo, there's one more thing that's bugging the hell out of me. To be honest, I've never felt so alone in my life. All I want to do is hide from everyone so I don't have to deal with my lousy performance and not being in the big leagues. It's all too much for me to handle."

The cats were out of the bag. No mystery remained about what was bothering him. It was time for Mark to take his hands off his throat and to stop choking himself to death.

An hour had now passed since we began talking. The tension that had coiled in Mark's body had receded, replaced with a kind of tranquility. Mark's face was relaxed, the wrinkles less defined, a sparkle returning to his eyes as he gained his composure.

"You know, I'm starting to feel a lot better. Maybe I just needed to get all this off my chest. I've been trying to act as if everything in my life is fine. But I guess it's time to let go of all the garbage I've stored in my head and get back to playing baseball."

"You should feel better. It's obvious you've been carrying around a lot of excess baggage, and avoiding your family and teammates is not the answer to your problems."

It was well past midnight when we walked back to the locker room. The only sounds in the stadium came from the cleanup crews on the graveyard shift. Before saying goodnight I said, "Mark, if you could have the rest of the season turn out any way you'd like, what would it look like? Just think about it."

The next day we returned to Vancouver to begin an eight-game homestand. I saw Mark when he entered the clubhouse. He had a peaceful look on his face, a spring in his step, and a little of the swagger I'd seen earlier when he was the best hitter in the league.

Later, on his way out to the field, Mark approached me. "Today's a new day," he barked. "I'm ready to take the rest of the season one day at a time."

That night Mark went 3-for-4, crushing line drives to all parts of Nat Bailey Stadium. His peashooter bat that I'd launched through the batting cage was now loaded with dynamite. The next night he exploded for four more hits, including a home run and two doubles. He continued his torrid pace over the next 10 days as he collected 25 hits in 40 at-bats. He was the hottest hitter in the league. The assault continued for the remainder of the season, allowing him to finish the season with a .340 batting average—second best in the league.

As I packed my bags after the last game, I took a few moments to reflect on the season just completed. I thought about the tremendous turnaround of Mark Dalesandro. Suddenly, a voice called me from behind. It was Mark's. "Hey, Mo, I just wanted to thank you for everything, especially that talk we had several weeks ago in Salt Lake City. It helped me with my hitting, but, more importantly it helped clear my mind."

Two hours later our team was in the airport saying their final goodbyes to another season. As I watched Mark Dalesandro disappear towards the plane that would take him home to Chicago, I couldn't help but think that baseball's struggles are not always due to physical or mechanical flaws. Sometimes, all that's required is an attitude adjustment.

"Whoever wants to know the heart and mind of America had better learn baseball, the rules and realities of the game."
—Jacques Barzun, God's Country and Mine, 1954

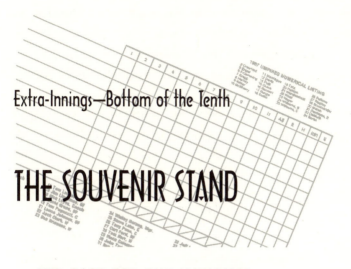

Extra-Innings—Bottom of the Tenth

THE SOUVENIR STAND

THE RACE FOR THE NATIONAL League Eastern Division title was on. Only a handful of games remained in the 1989 season as I strolled into the home clubhouse at Busch Stadium hours before the start of batting practice. I grabbed a pile of mail in my box and headed for a chair in the middle of the clubhouse.

For the most part, the letters held true-to-form—notes from fans interested in getting my autograph on either a baseball or index card. I scribbled my name on a couple of Topps and Fleer cards before I grabbed an envelope from the top of the pile. This one looked different. It was noticeably thicker, and strangely there was no return address. When I ripped it open, I was even more surprised that there were no cards to sign. I glanced at the first two lines and considered tossing it in the trash can. But something nudged at me. A gut feeling compelled me to keep reading.

And I'm glad I did. Here is the letter:

Dear John:

I have never written a fan letter or ever asked for an autograph (and don't want one now). Both have always seemed kind of senseless to me; my greatest idol was my dad until he died (I guess, now that I think about it, he still is and always will be), and I never got his autograph. But beside my father, my heroes have all been baseball players. I grew up on stories of the Gas House Gang; Enos Slaughter and Marty Marion were the gauges my parents used for defining the words "guts" and "effort." Baseball was really the only sport I could relate to, being a girl, and I remember spending my summer vacation days playing ball in the adjoining back yards (in an era when putting up a fence meant you were really pissed at your neighbor) pretending to be Mike Shannon or Julian Javier. If someone recorded a strikeout he could be Bob Gibson; if someone hit a long one he could be Roger Maris or Stan Musial. We would play ball all day long, usually pausing for a quick dinner break

(Photos by Rich Morris)

1969, eight-years-old. (Photos by Rich Morris)

and then resuming the game after, sometimes until our eyes strained to see the ball in the twilight. I grew up marking the advent of spring by two occurrences: the appearance of crocus blooms on the side of my parents' house, and the ten-day countdown till spring training. Baseball was to me the most glorious, most magical of sports, and the men who played the game were truly the boys of summer.

But a fan letter? Not likely. I may have been young and impressionable, but then I guess I was a bit cynical ("jaded" seems a strong word for a little girl), and I could never imagine a baseball player sitting on the bench reading with joy the accolades heaped on him by a kid. I still can't, so that probably brings about the question of why I'm doing it now as an adult. Well, it's a roundabout story.

During those days of pretending to be our favorite ballplayers, I thought I would love baseball (as I did my dad) forever. I thought it was something you were born with, this fierce emotion for a sport, and it would never go away. But I was wrong. Somewhere in the early 70s, maybe even as early as '69, I fell out of love. Tim McCarver in his book (and what a self-serving, whiny book it is) spends a couple of paragraphs in total bewilderment about the declining popularity of baseball in the 70s. I believe he called it "baseball bashing." All I can say is that perhaps a lot of people felt the way I did. I resented the fact that I could have reached base more times than some of those highly paid "boys,' and maybe the sight of my dad sitting at the kitchen table after eight or so hot, grimy hours at work, never complaining about his sprained knee or scuffed knuckles but still having the always ready smile for his kids, is what destroyed my love for baseball. I remember thinking that "real" baseball players had disappeared. I never saw the fire, the joy, or the competitiveness for any aspect but the contract in this new set of players. Maybe I felt betrayed or fooled. Whatever the reasons, the thrill was gone.

1975, eighth grade.
(Photo by Rich Morris)

1977, 10th grade—Mepham High School. (Photo by Rich Morris)

I can only explain it as a time warp of sorts. There is an eight-year or so time span when baseball barely existed. I did not watch a single complete game. Oh, I saw parts of games by accident. You couldn't have loved baseball like I had and not been drawn to the television if you happened to see Steve Carlton pitching or Mike Schmidt up to bat, and I have to admit I had a mild curiosity about the Philadelphia team in '79 and '80. But then pennant fever and the Series came to St. Louis in '82, and hidden beneath the outward careless attitude I exhibited for my more enthusiastic friends (I'd certainly call breaking into an impromptu rendition of "Celebration" in the middle of playing volleyball and nobody complaining) there was interest. I watched a couple of games, and as I watched Willie McGee, Keith Hernandez, and some of the others, I thought, "They make ballplayers like that again?" But when it was over, I considered it a fluke. There had been a glimmer there, a humming just beneath the surface, a faint reminder of what the game used to be and who used to play it. But I managed easily to forget about it again. I didn't miss it. Winter came and I watched hockey. (There was something in Dan Kelly's voice that, like Jack Buck's, lured you to the game.) Spring training came and went, and the season would have gone quietly to its grave in September without notice.

Except for a game on an August night in 1986. Okay, I'm guessing August, I'm reasonably sure it was Friday, but I'm positive it was at Shea (the Mets were just another ball team then, not pond scum yet). I was driving through Missouri and the only stations I could pick up clearly all the time were those from the small towns broadcasting Cardinals baseball. So I tuned in to the last couple innings. And it was like I was listening to the first game of my entire life.

It could have been the awe and excitement in Buck's voice as he described some magical feat of Ozzie Smith (who can resist Ozzie— okay, well, maybe some can). It may have been the memories that Buck's unique voice brought back to me of sitting on the front lawn pulling for our favorites. It might have been the pleasure of hearing one of my own favorites, Mike Shannon, had joined the broadcasting team. All I know is that I was hooked.

Freshman year, Seton Hall University, 1980. (Photo by Rich Morris)

And, of course, there's that other thing.

There was this "young man" they kept talking about and how he had been acquired from the Royals, that he was such a nice kid, and that he must be so thrilled to be playing in front of the hometown fans.

I don't know, maybe it was the idea of the "local kid makes good." But they spent an unusual amount of time, I thought, talking about a John Morris and how unique he was. Once a ball was hit long and the "nice young man" went back to nab it, and I caught in Buck's voice excitement that was normally reserved for Ozzie or Willie (and later on for Jack Clark). I wondered if there could really be someone in baseball who played the game because he loved it as much as the people who paid to watch it. I didn't think so, but I was curious, and it was worth it to begin watching the games and reading the sports page, and suddenly a door opened on a game that reminded me of my childhood. Friends began to watch me carefully. Here was this person one day sneering at ballplayers and talking about what a sissy sport it was (are you old enough to remember George Carlin's comparison of football and baseball?), and the next day she was checking the box scores.

It was wonderful. Like magic, like Houdini, baseball reappeared and left me wondering how it stayed gone that long. Have you ever lost something that you treasured, like a charm, and never expected it to be found, then miraculously one day it turns up. That's how it was for me. The boys of summer were alive and well and wearing Cardinal uniforms.

I found myself watching baseball being played by people more like my 60's team, players who gave everything to the game because they realized it was a fantasy come true. Like Ozzie Smith when he bounces off the turf to start a double play, or Jack Clark sending one out of the park as nonchalantly as he would walk out his front door and pick up the paper, or Keith Hernandez sucking up everything that came near first base. Men with beauty to their movements, whether it came naturally like to Darryl Strawberry or as a result of plain hard work like Howard Johnson. Men who are not so graceful but epitomize the spirit of the game, like Mickey Hatcher who redefines the words "effort" and "fire" when he ends up making plays that should be physically impossible for him.

And you? This might be hard for you to understand, but to me you represent everything fine and good about baseball. I've watched you

With batting coach Fred Hopke, Seton Hall University, Spring 1982. (Photo by Rich Morris)

play as if the entire future of baseball rested in your glove. I've seen you hydroplane on your ass 15 feet or so across puddles in the astroturf to make a catch. I've seen you drive in winning runs and then stand on first base like "no big deal" when I suspect that your heart is threatening to come crashing through your chest and you can't hear the crowd for the roaring in your ears. It was easy for me to feel sympathy when you lost your father (I had lost mine not so long before) but your understanding that what he wanted most was for you to play ball made me glad. When you were out with the injured back, it never occurred to me that you wouldn't be back (though I nearly passed out when you told a reporter that baseball wasn't the most important thing in your life; I'm fine now, thanks). The *Post-Dispatch* reported that you spent your own money to fly to St. Louis from Florida where you were rehabbing, to receive your pennant ring and I thought, how typical—this is no fluke, the guy just reeks with it. After rehab, your homerun in the '89 home opener was the only bright spot, a homecoming of sorts. I've seen you hovering like an eager child at the dugout steps (what do you think we do with those binoculars?) when your teammates were barely concealing their boredom on the bench, impatiently picking at the seams in your uniform, no doubt wondering when or if Whitey would put you in. I think I once caught you practicing an impression of a pitcher. I've had to laugh a couple of times when you whiffed on the ball, or sometimes when you enter the game in right field and you stand there prancing and wiggling like a horse in heat (your deep breaths are visible damn near into the upper decks). Once a friend and I shared a pair of binoculars and a good laugh when we watched you talk to a young girl behind the fence and then walk away with that certain walk men have when they know an attractive woman is watching (yes you do).

You are everything that is right about the game. Your spirit is the spirit of baseball.

In everyone's life there happens at least one time when a stranger touches their life in such a way that they didn't think possible. And then, if you're human, you feel that you have to let them know. So here it is. My thank you, John Morris. I don't know why I've sent it now, maybe it has to do with a feeling that your frustration might be building up and should know that it's not just Whitey and your teammates that consider you an integral part of the team. If you ever listen to KMOX, you must know that fans here in St. Louis appreciate you. You're doing well now, contributing when you're counted on, but I guess I just wanted you to know that even when slumps set in and things are looking bad, there are always some of us out here who appreciate you then too. When you're in a slump you don't have to make excuses unworthy of your ability. I can imagine the frustration that goes with watching your team losing a game and having one chance instead of four to help them. (Maybe you have an exceptionally strong character and really do think all the time that "what's best for the team is what matters." You probably do; that's one more reason for admiration.) But remember that your ability comes from within. You can do whatever you choose to do, and I would bet money on your one at-bat before I would on the bats of five others on the team I can name.

I haven't signed this letter because I do things on impulse sometimes that later on embarrass the hell out of me. And it doesn't matter who I am (we have not met), only what I am. A sincere fan. And not the kind that hunts you down and leaves deranged gifts on your front lawn.

Baseball is uncertain (I know—what a news flash). Down the road you might not be a Cardinal, and while that's a sad thought, maybe it will be better for you. Who knows, with the rumors of the new league beginning or expansion teams being granted, you might say good-bye to go play somewhere else everyday. In the meantime, let's hope things work out here. But remember, wherever you play, there will always be a fan in St. Louis who wishes you the best and is thankful for the gift you gave her. Good luck to you.

Five years away from the game now, I have a room full of trophies, shelves and boxes packed with autographed baseballs and bats, racks of team jerseys and jackets, and books full of newspaper clippings and photographs.

And then I have this letter.

ABOUT THE AUTHOR

John Morris began his professional baseball career in 1982, as a first-round draft pick of the Kansas City Royals after his junior year at Seton Hall University. He spent 12 years as an outfielder with the Kansas City Royals, St. Louis Cardinals, Philadelphia Phillies, and California Angels. In 1987, he was a member of the National League pennant-winning Cardinals. Following years of debilitating back injuries, John retired from active play in 1993 to become an instructor, coach, and manager in the Angels' minor league system.

Although he eventually left professional baseball altogether in 1996, John continues to put his major league experience to use as a motivational speaker and consultant to prominent collegiate baseball teams around the country. In 1994, he returned to Seton Hall to complete his degree in political science.

In addition, John and his wife Linda are successful independent Nikken distributors, a leading health care provider from Japan. Born in North Bellmore, New York, Morris resides in Gulfport, Florida. *"Bullet Bob" Comes to Louisville* is his first book.